TEST-TAKING STRATEGIES

Other Books by Judi Kesselman-Turkel and Franklynn Peterson:

BOOKS IN THIS SERIES

The Grammar Crammer: How to Write Perfect Sentences
Note-Taking Made Easy
Research Shortcuts
Secrets to Writing Great Papers
Spelling Simplified
Study Smarts: How to Learn More in Less Time
Test-Taking Strategies
The Vocabulary Builder: The Practically Painless Way to a Larger Vocabulary

OTHER COAUTHORED BOOKS FOR ADULTS

The Author's Handbook
The Do-It-Yourself Custom Van Book (with Dr. Frank Konishi)
Eat Anything Exercise Diet (with Dr. Frank Konishi)
Good Writing
Homeowner's Book of Lists
The Magazine Writer's Handbook

COAUTHORED BOOKS FOR CHILDREN

I Can Use Tools
Vans

BY JUDI KESSELMAN-TURKEL

Stopping Out: A Guide to Leaving College and Getting Back In

BY FRANKLYNN PETERSON

The Build-It-Yourself Furniture Catalog
Children's Toys You Can Build Yourself
Freedom from Fibromyalgia (with Nancy Selfridge, M. D.)
Handbook of Lawn Mower Repair
Handbook of Snowmobile Maintenance and Repair
How to Fix Damn Near Everything
How to Improve Damn Near Everything around Your Home

TEST-TAKING STRATEGIES

Judi Kesselman-Turkel and Franklynn Peterson

The University of Wisconsin Press

For Joe, starting a real life

The University of Wisconsin Press
1930 Monroe Street
Madison, Wisconsin 53711

www.wisc.edu/wisconsinpress/

3 Henrietta Street
London WC2E 8LU, England

5   4   3   2   1

Printed in the United States of America

Library of Congress Cataloging-in-Publication Data
Kesselman-Turkel, Judi.
Test taking strategies / Judi Kesselman-Turkel and Franklynn
Peterson.
    p. cm.
    Originally published: Chicago : Contemporary Books, c1981.
    ISBN 0-299-19194-X (pbk. : alk. paper)
    1. Test-taking skills. 2. Examinations-United States-Study
guides. I Peterson, Franklynn. II. Title.
LB3060.57.K36   2003
371.26-dc21   2003045823

CONTENTS

INTRODUCTION

Why You Need to Become Testwise

When you take a test—any test—you're really being tested on two things: how much you know about the subject and how much you know about taking a test.

Some people were born knowing how to throw a fastball. Some people seem to remember schoolwork without working at it. There are also some people who learn test-taking strategies without any outside help. They're not always the same people as the ones who learn information quickly. Yet they get the same high marks—sometimes higher.

With proper coaching and plenty of practice, anyone can learn how to throw a fastball. Our companion book, *Study Smarts*, shows how anyone can learn and remember schoolwork. This book describes how you can increase your test-taking ability—your "testwiseness," as behavior researchers call it—so you can compete on a par with your instinctively testwise classmates.

To begin, we will review a few of the more important principles of pretest studying. But if you need help in learning to study well, read *Study Smarts*. Most of *this* book is focused on how to take a test, because that's where the extra points that may change a C to a B or a B to an A really show up.

TEST-TAKING
STRATEGIES

1

Before-the-Test Study Strategies

Smart test-takers begin thinking about a test long before they enter the test room. In their heads or on paper, they compile a detailed profile of the test format and the test-giver. When they prepare for the test, they don't necessarily read and memorize every detail in their notes. They study specific kinds of information, in a specific way, for each individual kind of test. Finally, they get their minds, bodies, and emotions ready to give their all for high marks.

We'll show how to master all three of these important before-the-test strategies.

STRATEGY 1: FIND OUT WHAT KIND OF TEST YOU'RE GOING TO TAKE

Few students, except the ones who are instinctively test-wise, try to find out in advance what kind of test they're preparing for. But if you know the kind of test, you know how to study for it.

For short-answer, fill-in-the-blank, matching, and some

true-false tests, emphasis should be placed on cramming into your brain as many specific facts and details as possible. For essay or oral tests, you should prepare to argue persuasively about several general topics and to back up each argument with enough specific details to show that you probably know what you're talking about. For multiple-choice tests, you don't actually have to recall anything: you just have to recognize related information when you see it. In studying, you should look for those relationships.

As early in every course as possible, start compiling clues to what the exams will be like. Figure out the format.

- How much will be true-false statements?
- How much of the test will be multiple choice?
- How much will be essay?

And so forth.

Decide on the areas of knowledge.

- Will it include everything since the course began or only the last six weeks' worth?
- Will you have to remember formulas or will they be given?
- Will the textbook, outside reading, or lectures be given the most weight?

There are several ways to get this information.

Tactic 1: Ask the instructor

Many teachers are willing to tell you whether you'll be responsible for just plugging formulas into mathematical equations or for applying them to concrete situations. They'll state whether they expect details or just major concepts. They'll say whether they want just the facts and conclusions you've learned in class and from required reading, or expect your deductions and opinions. They'll also indicate whether or not they expect you to show that you've done outside reading.

Often, instructors will even tell you the format of their tests or the blocks of information and general subjects each test will cover. But many only tell the students who bother to ask. If you don't ask, you'll never know whether a testwise student is getting an informational edge on you.

Tactic 2: Look at past exams

If you've taken some tests in the course, you may already have a lot of clues about this coming test. Think about them.

- Was the teacher after straight memorization or did you just have to recognize the correct answers?
- Did earlier tests focus on trivia or on major principles?
- Did they include abstract questions or concrete ones?
- Did the teacher favor facts or ideas?
- Were the tests hand-scored or machine-scored—and by whom?
- Were there any catch questions? (If so, you'll have to watch for them this time around.)

Some teachers make available copies of past exams they've given. Study them for the types of questions you can expect. But don't fall into the trap of expecting identical questions or of anticipating the same format and then not reading the directions carefully once you're in the exam room. Instructors have been known to change a format or a particular question just *slightly*—with a word or two—as a trap for careless readers.

Tactic 3: Predict on past experience

If your teacher won't say a word about an upcoming exam and this is your first test given by the teacher, don't give up. Be testwise. Try to guess possible questions and format from the type of information emphasized in class, the focus of assignments, and the way the teacher presents the subject matter.

- Is the teacher a stickler for details?
- Does the teacher give greater value to facts or ideas?
- Which topics have been singled out for greater emphasis or more detailed explanation?
- Is the teacher the type who'll insert trick questions?
- Would the teacher care about weeding out the thinkers from the memorizers?
- What's the teacher's goal in teaching?
- What's the teacher's attitude toward testing?
- Will the teacher have the time—or make the time—to read essays?
- Are aides or teaching assistants available whom the teacher would trust to read essays?
- Is the teacher likely to choose a quick-scoring format?

Know your instructor. It'll tell you a lot about the exams.

STRATEGY 2: PICK A CRAMMING METHOD

There are two kinds of cramming for teacher-prepared tests: *intense cramming* and *prepared cramming*.

In *intense cramming* you begin—maybe only three days before the big exam—to start making some sense of the coursework. You do all the reading, make a pile of notes, and try to memorize like crazy until you have most of it shoehorned into your head. If you're a good crammer, almost everything you need to know will stay right at the top of your brain where, if you don't get so anxious that you forget it all, it'll last until the test is turned in. The morning after the test, you're practically guaranteed to wake up remembering very little of what you learned.

If you like standing on the edge of precipices, you can cram like this for almost any course in which you're convinced you'll never need any of the knowledge again. Most people can't do this with a foreign language, and it's not effective for a math course. But let's face it, once in awhile you just have to use this method; and at other times you may decide in advance that it's the best way. One of the authors once took an American Short Story course, read two 1,000-page books of stories in the week before finals, memorized forty or fifty titles, memorized authors' and main characters' names, memorized three-word plot summaries—and got an A. Two weeks later, of course, those American short stories were almost a complete blank.

You should keep in mind at least two other major shortcomings before choosing this *intense cramming* method.

1. If you're anxiety prone, this cramming program probably won't work even for short-term memory. Intense anxiety can cause large memory gaps during tests. The best remedy is self-confidence, and the surest way to achieve that is to practice *prepared cramming.*

2. Unless you're really desperate, don't use *intense cramming* for any course that contains information you'll need in a later course or that may have some value in helping you deal with life after college. *Prepared cramming* is a better, more lasting, and less ulcerating way to prepare for tests. In fact, if you've studied wisely all semester long, cramming should require no more than half a day—assuming that, about a week before the test, you start to seek help in those few areas that still give you trouble.

STRATEGY 2A: INTENSE CRAMMING—THREE-DAY CRAMMING FOR ONE-DAY REMEMBERING

Fortunately for people who put off studying until the last minute, there are only four steps in short-term, short-memory cramming.

Tactic 1: Single out the course's purpose

Guided by the course description or outline, write down the main topic as well as your instructor's purpose for teaching it. Examples: "American Business History—to show relationship between history of U.S. business sector and general U.S. history"; "Cellular Biology—cells as the building blocks of all life."

Tactic 2: Focus on the course's major topics

Using the course description, course outline, and any other aids you have such as textbook, class notes, outline series cram book, and anybody else's notes, list the topics of the course's major units. Under each main topic, list as many subtopics as the textbook or notes show.

Tactic 3: Make memory joggers

Now do your required reading, making the following notes as you go along.

1. For each subtopic, write a clear definition, explain how it ties into the overall purpose of the course, and jot down three specific examples.

2. Separately, but keyed to where they fit into your subtopic notes described above, list all names, dates, formulas, and other facts that seem significant and that you think you may be held responsible for on the test.

3. In a third place, list only those words you can't yet define but will have to recognize and define before exam time.

Example of notes for intense cramming

(1)

(2)

(3)

TEDDY ROOSEVELT STARTS SERIOUS GOV'T. REG. OF BIZ

Laws, regulations, licenses, lawsuits to watch over conduct of businesses.

Req'd. by overgreedy biz owners ("robber barons") who believed in "caveat emptor."

Examples:

1. Interstate Commerce Act (not effective)

2. Pure Food & Drug Act (quite effective)

3. Delaney Clause (modern— effective?)

MUST KNOW

Teddy Roosevelt = "trustbuster"

1887, Interstate Commerce Act

1890, Sherman Act

1903, U.S. Dept. of Commerce & Labor

1906, Hepburn Act

1906, *The Jungle*

1906, U.S. Meat Inspection Act

1920, "Rule of Reason" court decision

LEARN!!!

HEPBURN ACT
1. House = radical
2. Senate = innocuous law
3. U.S. rate regulation of railroads (i-state)
4. 1906
5. No free passes!
6. Sen. LaFollette —"not far enough"

THE JUNGLE
1. by Upton Sinclair
2. Socialist(?)
3. anti-caveat emptor
4. Chicago packing yards
5. "best-seller"
6. March 1906
7. Hero = Jurgis Rudkus (immigrant)

Tactic 4: Memorize the memory joggers

Use as many memorization techniques as you know in order to impress these facts and ideas on your memory. (Our book, *Study Smarts,* can help you with this.) If the exam is a fill-in-the-blanks or essay type, make sure you can spell unfamiliar words and can actively recall them, not just recognize them when you see them written out.

STRATEGY 2B: PREPARED CRAMMING—LONG-TERM CRAMMING FOR LONG-TERM REMEMBERING

This better, more relaxed way to cram assumes that you've been studying wisely all semester. By now you have condensed all your notes to a couple of pages—at most—that contain all the main ideas and facts you need to know for the exam. From those clue words, lists, charts, and diagrams, you'll be able to remember everything you've learned in the course. You're already familiar with the required new words, and you've learned their definitions. For foreign languages, you have word and phrase cards that you've made during the term as you've isolated the stumpers, as well as a list of regular verbs and a chart of irregular verbs organized according to patterns of ending. For technical courses, you may have cards with formulas on one side and their derivations on the rear and cards with equivalents that you're expected to know.

Your primary goal in this *prepared cramming* session is threefold:

(1) to get an overview of the coursework;
(2) to fit the facts and ideas into perspective; and
(3) to refresh your memory of the facts and associations, since everyone forgets part of what they've learned unless they review it at reasonable intervals.

There are three separate types of memory: recall, recognition, and association. For quick-scoring tests you'll need access to recognition and association. For essay and fill-in-the-answer tests you'll need all three.

There's a second goal in *prepared cramming:* to convince yourself that you're completely prepared for the exam. This will build your self-confidence, and self-confidence alone is often enough to erase most test anxiety.

Begin your prepared cramming session by taking an hour or so to organize your condensed notes, cards, and such. Then pull out the course outline you acquired or made at the beginning of the semester.

- Reread it for a total picture.
- Look for divisions into logical units, for trends, for relationships between ideas and between units.
- Summarize major findings and conclusions.
- Find the clues that show the relative importance of all the information you've learned. For instance, anything to which the instructor devoted extra time is probably important.

Now take an hour to rewrite your notes, actively trying to reorganize and condense them further so that they make the most possible sense. Check your memory as you go and leave out every fact and subordinate idea that you already know cold. Keep in writing only what you're not sure of and what you didn't understand the first time around. (If you're still having trouble understanding any of it, quickly make an appointment to consult the instructor or to get help from a qualified tutor.)

At this point you should have a page or two of main topics, along with memory prods such as significant names and dates. The night before the exam, go back over them. Overstudy: when you think you're 100-percent ready, study for another 25 percent of the time you've already devoted. Concentrate on the facts and ideas that you're having trouble with or that you tend to forget.

To get the most benefit from your prepared cramming, sleep *at least six hours* the night before the test. Researchers have shown not only that sleep of more than six hours' duration is the *best* solidifier of memorized material known to man, but also that if you get *less* than six hours of sleep, it has just the opposite effect, actually interfering with your memory.

STRATEGY 3: PRETEST

If past tests with their answer keys are available, use those questions as a pretest some time during the week before the exam. Otherwise, practice test-taking by making up an exam from past homework assignments.

Try to mimic the actual test situation as closely as possible. The best preparation of all is to take your pretest in the actual exam room, in the expected format, and during the same allotted time period. Researchers tell us that students raise their test scores just by being familiar beforehand with the test conditions.

It's especially important to set time limits for yourself so that you can learn to move along quickly. Every test is partly a test of how well you use your time.

STRATEGY 4: PREPARE EXTRA FOR PROBLEM-SOLVING

To prepare for exams in which you'll have to solve problems, copy one advanced problem from the textbook (if it supplies answers) or from past homework assignments for each important principle or law that you're responsible for knowing. (Usually, authors arrange problem sets in order of difficulty, so choose one toward the end of the group.) Then mix up the problems so that you can test whether or not you recognize them out of context and out of order.

Solve each problem and then check them all against the correct answers. You'll know very quickly just where your weak spots are. Correct your misconceptions—with help if you need it—and then do several more similar problems to reinforce your understanding.

STRATEGY 5: PREPARE EXTRA FOR UNFAMILIAR, QUICK-SCORING EXAMS

If you know that the test will have a type of question with which you're not familiar, or if you ordinarily stumble over that kind of format, try to find sample tests or past exams that use that particular format. (See Appendix A for suggestions for where to look.) Practice until you're convinced that you understand how to answer that type of question. Then, when you get into the exam room, you won't be thrown.

STRATEGY 6: PREPARE EXTRA FOR ESSAY EXAMS

After you've crammed for an essay exam, select eight or ten main topics based on the units in the course. For each topic or combination of several topics, make up one or two essay questions. One easy way is to tack on a word or two from the list in Appendix B; for example, "*Compare* and *contrast* the *X* main topic to the *Y* main topic."

Once you have the questions, jot down the outline you'd follow in writing each essay. (We'll discuss content and organization later.) But don't write the actual essay unless you need practice in writing.

STRATEGY 7: FORM A STUDY GROUP FOR ESSAYS AND ORALS

Unlike a tutor, who can be relied on to know what he's talking about if he's been recommended by a good source—instructor, department chair, or study skills center coordinator, for instance—the study group is just a collection of students who all want to get good test scores. Its main advantage is to help you think through your approach to the coursework out loud. You may also uncover some misunderstood facts and ideas when studying with a group, but it's important to consider that the wisest student may have incorrect information or zany ideas. So for best results, keep the following in mind.

When: Join a study group *after* you've learned the facts and ideas you need to know. That way, you won't learn incorrect information.

Why: The purpose of the group should be *conversation* that'll help you sharpen your long-term memory. You'll hone that memory more if you tell others what you know than if you sit back and listen to *them.* You'll also learn better by having to explain your ideas coherently.

How: Any method that will get you thinking and talking about your facts and ideas is a good method. To help you focus on ideas, ask one another questions that could be on the essay exam. Here's one very effective technique. Each member of the group prepares five essay questions in advance and then each person prepares answers and discusses them.

Where: Choose a place where there are no distractions so that the group can give its entire attention to the subject. And choose someplace where the group's enthusiasm won't be dampened by someone saying, "Tone it down," in the background.

How long: An advantage of study groups is that they

often make even a dull subject interesting. That will help your memory. On the other hand, there's a tendency to sidetrack into talk about dates or football scores. One hour spent with everyone's mind on the subject is worth four hours of work with time-outs every few minutes for fun and games.

Who: Anyone, as long as he or she understands the point of the study group, can participate. The point is not to teach but to discuss facts and ideas that are already learned, not to socialize but to study. Study groups help slow students put together relationships between facts. They make bright students aware of how most students think, and show them why test preparers like straightforward, obvious answers. They help inarticulate or shy students become more articulate. They help everyone prepare for both essays and oral exams.

2

What to Do About Before-the-Test Worry

If test marks didn't count, nobody would worry about tests. But they do count, and most of us do worry. In fact, those who don't worry at all actually don't do as well as they would if they did worry a little.

Some worry, researchers show, is good for us. It sharpens our alertness. It's only when you worry a lot that you start to lose test points. The worry then interferes with your memory, driving clear out of your mind the things you knew yesterday like the back of your hand.

Other emotions can also hurt your memory and your test marks: anger, depression, and lack of confidence. So it's as important to prepare emotionally for a test as it is to prepare all the information you need. In fact, for standardized tests, it's often practically the only kind of preparation you can make.

STRATEGY 1: BOLSTER YOUR CONFIDENCE

If you have taken any psychology courses, you've heard

about the "self-fulfilling prophecy"—the tendency to do as well, or as poorly, as you expect to do. This is particularly true for exams. If you feel confident about passing, you'll lose some of your anxiety about the test. If you believe that you are going to do well, you will. Testwise students gain points just because they have confidence.

So, do everything you can to bolster your confidence. Study the coursework so that you're 125 percent sure of it. Get a tutor to quiz you if you need someone else's judgment that you know your stuff. Forget about the brightest student in the class; he's surely not losing confidence worrying about you. Keep your mind on showing how much *you* know.

Just don't become so overconfident that you become careless. Remember, a little worry is good for you.

STRATEGY 2: MINIMIZE DISCOMFORT

Visit the test room beforehand so that it will be familiar to you by test time. Sit in a seat you like. Actually do some homework there. Students really do perform better when they take a test in the room in which they studied for it.

Notice whether the room is cold or warm so you can dress comfortably for the test. Notice the distractions in the room and eliminate as many of them as you can. For example, if there's an interesting wall chart, study it now so that you won't be tempted to do so during the test.

If you know who your proctor will be, it might also help to meet that individual beforehand so that you'll feel there's a friend in the exam room, not an enemy.

STRATEGY 3: GET HAPPY

Many students roll through college in a constant manic-depressive cycle, up some days and down some days. A lot of this emotional volleying can't be prevented. Still, the happier you can feel when you're entering the exam room, the better you'll score.

For a week or so beforehand, avoid depressing situations and seek out enjoyable ones. Postpone asking that someone for a date unless you're sure the answer will be yes. Treat yourself to a ticket to the rock concert you're dying to see. Buy the sweater that you've had your eye on for weeks. Get happy.

STRATEGY 4: SHAKE YOUR ANGER

Whether you are angry at your roommate for throwing a party the night you were planning to study or at an instructor for switching test formats at the last minute, convince yourself that it's not worth losing points over. Shake your anger before you go into the test room, or it will end up lowering your grades.

If your anger is caused by a feeling that tests are unfair and test questions are badly written, it may be because you lack test-taking skills. This book should help you eliminate that problem.

STRATEGY 5: WORRY ONLY ABOUT WHAT'S REAL

If you haven't studied at all for the course, you ought to be frightened of the test. There is no magic formula to eliminate valid fear.

But if you have gone to past tests prepared and still haven't done well on them, it's probably because you haven't learned the test-taking strategies other students use. You may not be aware of how many points you lose against competitors who are testwise. Read on, and we'll help you reap those extra points. Then you will have nothing to worry about.

STRATEGY 6: KNOW WHEN TO POSTPONE

Sometimes it's a good idea to postpone a test if you can. If your body is fighting physical illness, it will lower your grade.

It has also been demonstrated that some women don't do as well on tests just before menstruation, and if you know that you're among them, postponement is sometimes sensible.

But you should never postpone a test because of fear or anxiety, unless it's because you don't know the work and you're sure you can learn it thoroughly between now and postponement day. What you put off now due to anxiety only leads to even greater anxiety—and even poorer performance—when you finally do have to take the test.

STRATEGY 7: GET HELP FOR TERROR

Some people are the victims not just of fear but of irrational test terror. If you have nightmares about taking tests, go blank or actually black out when you walk into an exam room, become physically sick before every test, or miss most tests through oversleeping, it's important to get professional help from a school psychologist.

Just as special allowances are made for people with other types of handicaps, people who are emotionally incapable of handling large-group test situations should be given alternative kinds of exams. Why don't you offer a convincing alternative yourself? You might offer to write an extra paper or make a special presentation. Or you might do a take-home exam that is more difficult than the original test would have been. Perhaps the teacher would permit you to take the test in his or her office or with a Teacher's Assistant.

One way of dispelling irrational fears has met with some success. First, imagine the test situation that you fear and then imagine yourself in it, taking the test with no fear, no worry, no racing heart. Imagine yourself sailing through it, knowing all the answers. Imagine yourself getting the best mark in the entire test group. Try to remember a situation in which you did well on an exam and keep remembering that experience over and over, reliving it as closely as your imagination allows. Now connect these good thoughts with thoughts of the upcoming test. Do this over and over in your mind. That's called *positive reinforcement*.

Practice this technique, and some of the good feelings really will carry over into the actual exam. If you do find anxiety creeping up on you, take a deep breath and refocus on that good feeling. Then go on with the test.

3

What to Do in the Test Room

STRATEGY 1: GET INTO THE MOOD

Just as your emotional attitude *before* the test influences
how well you prepare for it, your emotional state *during* the
test can determine whether or not you do your best. We have
found six ways you can use to get yourself into the best test-
taking mood.

Tactic 1: Don't fight it

Sure, there are lots of reasons to resist tests. They classify
students. They categorize people. They often unfairly reward
students who memorize and penalize people who analyze.
Conformity is an asset on tests, but creativity is often a
liability.

The trouble is that you will get a higher mark if you can
convince yourself that a test *does* count, that it's really worth
your best effort. If you can't work up some enthusiasm for

the idea of showing how much you know, then try imagining what A's can do for your career. And if that doesn't impress you, deliberately focus on something that does.

Tactic 2: Get to the test room early enough to relax

Being a bit keyed up helps, but being uptight or feeling rushed can cost you points. Get to the exam room a few minutes early so that by the time the test begins, you are relaxed and comfortable in your surroundings. However, don't arrive so early that you'll have time on your hands to work yourself into a panic.

Here's a relaxation technique that will help you loosen up your body and your mind. Practice it first in your own room, then in a room at the library, and finally in the actual test room a day or two before the exam, if possible. Once you have mastered the technique, you'll be able to use it even during the actual test.

1. Get comfortable in your chair.

2. Now tense every muscle in your body—and keep it tensed—starting with your head and working down your body. Concentrate on how each muscle feels as you progress. First tense your *forehead* by scowling, then your *neck* by pulling in your chin, then your *back* by squeezing your shoulders down. Pull your *stomach* up against your ribs, tighten your *lower back,* stretch out your *fingers,* knot your *upper leg muscles,* and then your *calves.* Stretch your *feet* and finally your *toes.* By now you should be as stiff as a board—all over.

3. Next, relax each set of muscles that you just tensed. Start with your toes and work upward. Pay attention to how each muscle feels as you relax it, and keep all the muscles relaxed as you move upward. Concentrate on how you feel as the tension leaves your muscles one by one. When you get to your chest muscles, breathe deeply several times and

continue breathing deeply as you finish the relaxation procedure. As you breathe, notice how you exhale all the tension.

4. After you have practiced this relaxation exercise a dozen or so times you'll be able to spot which muscles are the ones you generally tense up under pressure. Those should be your signal muscles, the ones that cue you, "Hey, you're getting uptight. Take a minute to relax."

5. As soon as you are comfortable in the exam room, go through the entire relaxation technique once. After that, simply watch for signs of tension in your signal muscles. At that point, some people go through the entire relaxation technique, which takes less than a minute; others simply tense the signal muscles fully, then deliberately relax them while breathing away the tension.

Tactic 3: Concentrate

If you can block out all distractions and concentrate only on the test, not only will you finish faster but you will lose fewer points for careless mistakes. So it's important that you expose yourself to as few distractions as possible.

- Take a seat away from the windows so you won't be as tempted to look at people passing by outside.
- Take a seat away from the aisles so you won't pay attention to students leaving the room early. (The first people out of a test room, it's been shown, are usually the ones who have failed. So don't make the mistake of comparing your time to theirs.)
- Stay away from friends and classmates who are so attractive as to be distracting.
- If the room is poorly lit, sit right under a light fixture.
- If the door is open and it gets noisy outside, ask the proctor to close it. It is the proctor's job to create optimal test conditions for everyone. (If the proctor

won't close it, try to forget it. Don't let the situation disturb you.)

- You have been told since grade school to bring enough pencils or pens or whatever else you'll need for an exam. Also bring some candy bars so you won't be distracted by thoughts of hunger.
- Bring a sweater so you won't think about being chilly.
- Bring a watch so you won't keep looking up at the clock and possibly become distracted by something going on in your line of sight. (If you don't own a watch, borrow one. If the room doesn't have a clock, test-takers with watches will have a decided advantage.)

STRATEGY 2: DON'T LET TEST-TAKING ANXIETY GET YOU DOWN

Most of us worry at least a little during a test, but some worry more than others. Psychologists who have studied those people call them "test anxious." Researchers now tell us that if your anxiety gives you an upset stomach or a racing heart, you may feel uncomfortable but it probably *won't* affect your test scores. So if you have this kind of test anxiety, the best way to deal with it is to treat it like any other kind of distraction—ignore it. The less attention you pay to it, the less you'll feel it and the faster you'll return to solving problems successfully on your test.

On the other hand, if you frequently have great difficulty coping with text anxiety, you may need stronger medicine than just the assurance that it's not going to affect your test grades. We suggest you turn back to Chapter 2: What to Do About Before-the-Test Worry.

STRATEGY 3: THINK BEFORE YOU POP A PILL

We've known some students who swore so completely by

pep pills and tranquilizers that it seemed as if they thought the pills contained all the knowledge they needed to pass an exam. For some students in some situations, pills do help. For most, the disadvantages outweigh the advantages.

Pep pills can help some people by making them seem more alert. If you've gotten too little sleep, they will keep you awake. But they won't help you concentrate. In fact, they may make it harder to think through complicated problems from beginning to end.

Tranquilizers generally have the opposite effect. If you are overly anxious, they may help you relax, though they have been shown to be of minimal help to younger students. But you'll give up some alertness in return for tranquility. In some people, they also decrease motivation, and a desire to do well is a strong tool in helping you actually do well on an exam.

Don't try either pep pills or tranquilizers for the first time during or even just before an exam. First know how they affect your own particular metabolism. Then weigh the losses against the gains.

STRATEGY 4: DUMP YOUR WORRIES ONTO PAPER

Many students spend a lot of time worrying about whether or not they will be able to recall all the names, dates, formulas, and other facts they're sure they'll need on an exam. It would be so easy if they could just take a set of notes with them into the exam room.

Of course, you generally can't. However, there's nothing to prevent you from doing the next-best thing. As soon as the test is handed out, jot down in some convenient corner of the paper everything you're afraid you may forget during the test. This may consume a minute or two of time, but by dumping onto paper all those little worries that would be swimming around inside your head, you'll be able to concentrate more effectively on the rest of the exam.

STRATEGY 5: PUSH ON!

Good test-takers get themselves keyed up to perform as fast as they can while still being careful and thorough. They don't stop to reconsider a problem. Even on a test that they expect to finish early they *push on* because they know that the mind works best when it is under some pressure.

In later chapters of this book we will offer some specific tips about how to use your test time most effectively. One general rule that applies to nearly all situations is: "Push on!"

4

How to Do Your Best on Any Kind of Test

Testwise students use most of the following general test-taking strategies without thinking. With a bit of thinking, you can make them part of *your* bag of test tricks.

STRATEGY 1: GET THE MOST CREDIT IN THE LEAST TIME

Time isn't always a problem in taking tests. But you should find out at the beginning whether or not it might be. If it is, then you need a plan to make the best use of your time.

Tactic 1: Decide whether to speed or not to speed

Take a minute to skim the test. Decide whether it's a speed test or an accuracy test. Most standardized tests are speed tests; only the very few top performers are expected to be able to finish the test. On the other hand, most course tests are accuracy tests; the tester expects that everyone who is a C student or above will be able to finish the test without rushing.

Tactic 2: Budget your time

Right at the beginning, allocate your time. And stick to your allocations! Standardized tests often do this for you by giving you fifteen or twenty minutes for each section, after which you're supposed to go on to the next section. You will actually answer the most questions, and get a higher score if you follow those instructions. Since speed-test preparers don't expect most people to get to every question, don't be thrown if you don't complete each section.

For course tests, divide up your time according to how many points each item is worth. For example, if one question or one section is worth 50 percent of your score, plan to spend half your time on it. (Of course, if you don't use the entire time allotted for any particular question, move on to the next one right away.)

Tactic 3: Take the easy questions first

If you don't have to answer questions in order, and there are relatively few questions on the test, pick out the easy ones. Get them out of the way first. This will calm your anxiety and, at the same time, get your memory working smoothly. But don't waste time trying to sort out the difficult questions from the easy ones; allow yourself no more than a few minutes.

Tactic 4: Read all the essay questions in advance

On essay tests in which you can choose, say, three out of

five questions, read all the choices first. Then make your selection based on which ones you can answer best within the allotted time. If you have to choose four, for example, but only know answers for three of them, go ahead and write those three. Then review the remaining possibilities. Writing the three essays may have triggered enough of your memory to allow you to do a good job on one other topic.

Tactic 5: Leave the time-wasters for last

If you seem to be taking too much time on one particular question, stop working on it. Mark it so that you'll be able to find it easily after you've tackled the other questions. Then move on. If you have time left over at the end of the test, you can go back to the marked question; by that time another question or answer may have sparked your memory on the earlier problem. If you don't have leftover time, you will have scored more points for correctly answering twelve questions that came easily to you than only nine that you sweated over.

Avoid skipping too many questions, because rereading them will also waste time. We suggest that you try not to skip more than one out of every ten questions.

Tactic 6: Check your watch

Look at your watch at sensible intervals to make sure you aren't falling behind. One workable plan is to check the time after every test section, another to look after every quarter of the test is finished. If you know from past tests that you tend to be slow, start by checking the time more frequently; that can help you develop a quicker rhythm. But don't let worry about time distract you from concentrating on the answers.

Tactic 7: Use all the time

Students who walk out of the test room early are often cheating themselves out of time they could use to good advantage. Reread the questions as well as your answers. Check for accuracy, legible writing, and questions you may have missed. Erase stray marks on machine-scored tests. On standardized tests, even if the directions say otherwise, test-wise students often go back to earlier sections.

STRATEGY 2: GIVE THEM WHAT THEY ASK FOR

A University of Chicago study showed that one thing most clearly separates testwise students from the rest: how accurately they read the directions and the questions. It's not that the testwise students are better readers; they just know what to look for. Here's how you too can understand what the directions and questions really ask for.

Tactic 1: Read critically

Read all directions and all questions as slowly and carefully as necessary. Don't jump to the conclusion that they're the same old instructions or questions you've seen in class or on earlier tests. Be especially alert for words that may slightly change what is being asked this time from what you have seen before. Watch for punctuation that can change the meaning of phrases in the instructions. Be sure you don't read "and" where the instructions say "or," or read "have to" where instructions say "may." Be careful not to read your own meanings into questions or instructions.

Tactic 2: Flag tricky directions

If some of the test instructions look tricky, circle or underline their key words. For example, if the directions say "blacken in the correct square" and you circle the words *blacken in*, you won't turn in a paper that is answered with check marks. On machine-scored tests, blacked-in spaces always register; with checks, you can never be sure that you will get credit for correct answers.

If your test includes an answer booklet or work paper, actually jot down important instructions such as "answer three essay questions out of five," "show all calculations," "two from Part A, one from Part B," and "copy the question." If the directions are complicated, number each step you have to take. Then remember to look back occasionally at the key phrases and steps. (On the other hand, don't keep rereading questions or directions needlessly; if your underlines or clue words are adequate, you can check yourself in just a few seconds.)

Tactic 3: Flag complicated questions

If questions are complicated, break them down into manageable parts. Number each part so you can check quickly to be sure that you have answered all the parts.

Tactic 4: Use all the help you can get

If directions say that you can use aids such as calculator, scrap paper, or even textbooks, don't play hero. Use them. You can be sure that testwise people are using them.

Tactic 5: Don't skip sample questions and answers

If sample questions and answers are given, as they often are in standardized tests, work them through. They will tell you whether the tester expects you to answer the questions with obvious answers or with thoughtful ones. They will also demonstrate how you're expected to *mark* your answers.

STRATEGY 3: WATCH OUT FOR CARELESS ERRORS

It's disheartening to work out a problem just right and get no credit for it because of some silly mistake you made in writing down the answer. Here's a quick checklist to use during every exam.

Tactic 1: Double-check when the pressure is off

Save time at the end of the exam to look for careless errors. Under tension, we all make slips. At the end of the test, when the pressure's off, we can usually find most of them.

- Reread questions to make sure that you read them accurately.
- Reread answers to make sure that you wrote what you meant to write.
- Be sure that all your numbers are legible.
- Double-check your calculations, using an alternate calculating method if possible.

Tactic 2: Fill in the right blanks

Make sure that you have put your name on the test—on all separate parts of the test. And be sure that you have placed all the answers in the proper spots. This is especially important to check when questions are on one sheet and answers on another.

Tactic 3: On essays, don't waste space

Don't skip lines, or cover only one side of a page (unless so directed), or use ornate handwriting on essays. First of all, you just might run out of space. Getting another test booklet takes up valuable time. Besides, test-graders might look on space-wasting as your way of trying to cover up for not knowing the material—and *that* can cost you points.

STRATEGY 4: TRY TO REASON OUT ANSWERS TO TOUGH QUESTIONS

Testwise students know that there's a large gray area between *knowing* and *not knowing* an answer. They don't give up if they're stumped at first; they try to reason through the question systematically. Here's how you can do the same.

Tactic 1: Look for clues in the question

Don't ever assume that you can't answer a question simply because the contents seem unfamiliar at first. Try to substitute more concrete words or numbers for abstract ones. For example, if you encounter the term *production isoquant* on an exam and draw a blank, notice how *isoquant* divides into two possible stem words. *Quant* generally has something to do with *quantity,* doesn't it? Now, what about *iso? Iso*therms on a weather map are lines connecting points of *equal* temperatures. *Iso*sceles triangles have two *equal* sides. So *isoquant* might mean equal quantities. See if this definition helps you answer the test question.

Tactic 2: Look for clues in the answer choices

When several answer choices are given, you can often reason out which answer is best. (In Chapter 5, on multiple-choice test strategies, we discuss this reasoning tactic in great detail.)

Tactic 3: Keep your eyes open for memory joggers

If one question stumps you, keep it filed away in the back

of your mind as you go through the rest of the exam. Very often a question or answer that you haven't reached yet will trigger your memory on the earlier question. If you encounter enough related questions, maybe you can figure out in which chapter or lecture the stumper was given, and that can jog your memory.

Tactic 4: Save tough questions for last

Sometimes you don't need clever clues to figure out answers to questions that stumped you the first time through. Very often, it was tension that made your mind go blank; the relaxation that comes from getting through the entire test can frequently resurrect the right answer for you.

Tactic 5: If all else fails, guess

Except on exams that deduct a lot of points for incorrect answers, smart test-takers make educated guesses until they have filled in all the blanks. As a general rule:

- guessing *always* pays off when no points are deducted for it;
- guessing *nearly always* pays off in a course test for which you have studied, because when you have studied, you will rarely encounter a question about which you know absolutely nothing;
- guessing *definitely* pays off, even if points are subtracted for wrong answers, when you're given choices from which to select your answers.

How can you tell whether points are deducted for guesses? If the test directions tell you to answer all the questions, you can assume there will be no penalty for guessing. On standardized and other tests that give you a score sheet to work on, see if there is a space for the grader to list the number of wrong answers. If so, you should limit guessing to the questions for which the odds seem to be in your favor. (In later chapters we'll talk about how to make educated guesses on specific kinds of tests.)

STRATEGY 5: GET SPECIAL CLUES FROM STANDARDIZED TESTS

Standardized tests are generally designed in standard ways. Testwise students learn how they are designed and use that information to get better scores. They all apply the following tactics.

Tactic 1: Remember that questions proceed from easy to difficult

Questions within particular sections usually progress in difficulty. So if you meet a difficult question at the beginning, you're probably reading too much into it or missing something obvious. On the other hand, if an easy question seems to be near the end, you're probably missing a subtlety or falling for a trick; reread the question more carefully.

Tactic 2: Fill in all the blanks

Standardized tests are usually time tests. (See Strategy 1 in Chapter 1.) That means that very few people will finish all the questions. If you deliberately save a bit of time for the end of the test, you can go back and fill in *all* the blanks quickly. Since an unanswered answer is sure to be wrong, *any* answer can only help you get a better score.

Tactic 3: Remember the odds

Even on tests that subtract quarter-points for wrong answers, with educated guessing you may be able to play the odds and come out ahead. For example, many tests with four-part multiple-choice questions have two choices that are usually obviously wrong; even a flip of the coin on the remaining two choices results in the right answer two out of four times. And if you let your instincts and other clues help pick out the right choice among the two possibilities, the percentages climb way above three out of four.

STRATEGY 6: GET SPECIAL CLUES FROM INSTRUCTOR-PREPARED TESTS

Instructors who prepare tests generally have distinctive styles and particular patterns in mind. Here's how to find them and let them guide you to making educated guesses.

Tactic 1: Don't look too hard for hidden meanings in questions

Instructors tend to mix up easy and difficult questions, but they aim the questions at the level of understanding of average students. So don't read *extra* meaning into ordinary questions.

If two answers look correct, give the most obvious answer. (If there is room on the answer sheet, point out the question's ambiguity or indicate how the other answer might also be correct. If there is no room or no time to do this, take it up with the teacher *before* you get your graded test paper back.)

If no answer seems correct, choose the one that is most nearly correct. (Again, if you have time as well as room on the answer sheet, point out the discrepancy. If not, take it up with your teacher before the test grades are given back.)

Tactic 2: Look for clues within the questions

Instructor-prepared exams are usually full of valuable clues. Learn where to look for them.

Teachers try to use good grammar in the correct answers but often aren't as careful with the incorrect ones. If the question is in the past tense, but three of the four multiple-choice answers are in the present tense, the one in the past tense is likely to be the correct answer. (But if you've got a trickster for a teacher, watch out!)

Very often, the answer to one problem is contained in a later question. Keep your eyes open for this.

5

Multiple-Choice Test Strategies

Multiple-choice is the most popular kind of standardized test. It's popular with professors, because the answers are easy for teaching assistants to grade. And it's the type of exam that rewards testwise students with the most extra points for their testwiseness.

We have arranged the strategies for answering multiple-choice questions in the order in which you should use them during an exam. In other words, if strategies 1 through 3 supply the answers, don't even bother to use strategies 4 through 9.

STRATEGY 1: WORK QUICKLY

Studies have shown that students who rapid-fire their way through multiple-choice tests—even if they pick some answers at random—get better scores than students who may know the material better but are slow at taking tests.

Read each question through just once. Don't dawdle

about putting down the right answer the instant you come to it. If you have second thoughts about the answer, don't stop to think about it right then; jot down a little mark alongside the number. Then, if you have time at the end of the test, you can go back and think over your first answer.

If an answer seems obvious, have confidence in yourself. Choose that simple answer. Don't waste time looking for hidden qualifications and tricks.

STRATEGY 2: GIVE THE ANSWER THE TEACHER WANTS

Sloppy reading and intellectual heroics can cost you test points. Learn to read—and to understand—test instructions as well as questions. Then follow them.

Tactic 1: Make sure you understand precisely what the directions tell you to do

Some tests, especially teacher-prepared versions, ask for the *most correct* answer. In that case, you may have to figure out more than just the answer; you may have to figure out what the test preparer's biases are. Remember, it's not what seems most correct to *you* that counts, but what the *teacher* believes is most correct. This is not the time to stand staunchly by your own opinions.

Some teacher-made tests allow for *more than one* correct answer. If you're supposed to mark *all* the right ones, be sure to do it.

Be careful on tests that include "all of the above" or "none of the above" choices. Don't select a choice like that unless it applies *totally*. For example, if the first two choices are right, the third choice is definitely wrong, and the fourth choice is "all of the above," *don't* check off number 4. Choose between number 1 and number 2.

Tactic 2: Study the "given" part of each question

Read quickly, but read *every* word that counts. (If you're not good at this, practice. Race against the clock using the practice test books listed in Appendix A. This is a skill that can be learned. Learn it.)

If the "given" section of a question (test-designers call it the *stem*) includes several complicated statements, isolate each of them. Make sure you understand each individual part. When you have picked an answer, check it against each segment. Your answer has to satisfy every part of the question. Several studies have shown that this knack of breaking down complicated questions into several smaller ones rewards testwise students with extra points on almost every exam.

STRATEGY 3: GUESS BEFORE YOU CHOOSE

Figure out your answer before you look at the possible choices. If it's among the choices, you'll save a lot of time. If it isn't, forget it and start studying each of the choices. At least you will have activated the part of your memory that applies to the topic, and that can help you recognize the answer your test-maker is seeking.

STRATEGY 4: CHOOSE THE CLOSEST ANSWER

Most multiple-choice tests look for the quick, easy response. By their very nature, they are simplistic. So choose the closest answer—even if you think it isn't 100 percent correct.

If a test is well constructed, all the answers will seem somewhat plausible. In that case, there will probably be at least one clue word in the stem that makes one answer definitely better than all the rest. Go back and reread the stem, looking for that clue word.

Some test-makers set traps for the unwary. They may put a plausible but incorrect choice first, then surround the one correct answer with some implausible choices. So don't grab at answer (a) until you have read (b), (c), and (d) as well.

STRATEGY 5: ELIMINATE IMPLAUSIBLE ANSWERS

The greater the number of ridiculous choices you can discard, the better your odds are of choosing the correct answer.

- Some answers are obviously wrong. Move quickly to the next possibility.
- Many answers are partly wrong. If they are wrong in *any* significant way, they're not the right choice unless the question was badly written. In that case, take it up with your instructor *after* the exam but *before* grades are given out.
- Many answers are correct statements by themselves. But they have nothing to do with the stem part of the question. Don't get trapped into choosing one of these.
- Sometimes two answers say exactly the opposite thing. In such a case, the correct answer is usually one or the other of the pair. (But if your teacher is a trickster, be wary!)
- Many times, two of the answers are similar. Often only one or two words are different. Again, the correct answer is usually one of the pair. Decide how the two answers are different and how these differences make one correct and the other incorrect.

STRATEGY 6: LOOK FOR CLUE WORDS OR NUMBERS

You can't always figure out correct answers by looking for

clue words. In fact, some clever test-makers deliberately insert phony clues to throw the unwary student off the track. But if you have exhausted the first five strategies, then give this one a try. Looking for clues may point you to an answer that you suddenly remember as the correct one.

Tactic 1: Watch for absolutes and qualifiers

Answers that include *always, never, all,* and *none* are often incorrect. Few things in life are *always* true or *always* false. Test-designers who try to avoid quarrels over the answers like to slip in qualifiers such as *seldom, generally,* and *tend to be.*

Here's an actual exam question that could have been figured out using this method:

> All of the following theories about the state of the dead are represented in the *Odyssey* except:
> 1. The dead may be changed into minor gods and thus achieve immortality.
> 2. The fortunate dead go to fields of eternal summer.
> 3. The spirits of the dead are taken to the Underworld.
> 4. Death is simply the end, with no survival in any form.

Got it all figured out already. No? Well, in number 1 the tester says, "The dead *may be* changed. . . ." Number 2 says, "The *fortunate* dead go. . . ." In number 3 you won't find such easy clue words, but anyone who knows anything about Greek mythology recognizes the statement as being true. Notice that in number 4 the clue words give it all away: ". . . *no* survival in *any* form." That's right. The correct answer is number 4. Even if you had never opened the *Odyssey,* if you used Strategy 6 you could get the correct answer!

Tactic 2: Look for grammatical clues

As we mentioned in the previous chapter, there's a tendency among test-makers to have the correct answer agree grammatically with the stem; they seldom take such care with incorrect responses. But beware: this is also a favorite trick of testers who like to throw testwise students off the track.

Tactic 3: Look for familiar phrases

In teacher-prepared tests, stems and correct responses are often taken right out of textbook or lecture notes. So if you recognize particular words or phrases—or if the stem and one answer just naturally flow smoothly together in your mind—follow your hunch.

Tactic 4: Look for degrees of correctness

If the answer is a number, at least one choice is likely to be too large and one too small. If time is involved, one date is likely to be too early, one too late.

However, if one possibly correct choice is very specific, and another possibly correct choice is very general, the general one may be the one you want. This is especially true if the general choice incorporates all or most of the information in the specific choice.

None of these clues is foolproof, of course. But they are a lot more dependable than wild guessing!

STRATEGY 7: GUESS

On four-part multiple-choice tests, random guessing on all of the questions would give you an average grade of 25 percent. But you rarely need to guess randomly. On most multiple-choice tests, you should quickly be able to rule out two of the four possible answers by using what you *do* know plus the strategies we have already presented in this section. That alone can result in an average grade of 75 percent achieved by guessing alone. If you also use a bit of intelligence, you can push the guess rate beyond 80 percent.

We know someone who got stuck in a required ROTC course. Staunchly, he refused to read the textbook. On the other hand, he didn't want to flunk the course; he would just have had to take it over. He noticed that all the exam questions were four-part multiple choices and that two parts were always ridiculous. So he flipped a coin on the remaining choices and ended up with exactly 75 for his grade. We don't recommend this, but it shows how well the method works.

If you draw a total blank on the test's information, you still may be able to slant the odds in your favor. *Watch for patterns in the answers.* Some large-scale hand-corrected tests actually use definite answer patterns to simplify scoring. So. if all else fails, if answer (c) hasn't been chosen on your answer sheet for a long time, fill in (c). Unless you're penalized for wrong answers, *any* answer is better than *no* answer.

STRATEGY 8: DO CHANGE ANSWERS

A popular old wives' tale says, "Never change an answer." Don't follow this adage. Research shows that when you have a hunch that you ought to change an answer, your hunch usually proves to be right. But follow your hunches systematically.

- Don't go over answers until you have finished the test. Then use all the time you have.
- First, go back and reread the directions. Make sure you've followed them to the letter.

- Next make sure you have put all your answers in the correct places. You'd be shocked at how many students lose lots of points for not checking this.
- Next check over the questions and answers that you flagged for further thought.
- Finally, if you still have time, go over all your other answers.

If you believe that you ought to change an answer, change it. Sometimes just answering all the questions will give you clues—consciously or unconsciously. Also, by the end of the test you should have a better understanding of the test-maker's point of view; maybe you can figure out what he or she was driving at in a poorly worded question.

Don't keep changing answers back and forth. Repeated changes of the same answer rarely pay off; they just waste time.

Before you hand in your paper, be sure to erase all marks that don't belong on it.

STRATEGY 9: NEVER GIVE UP!

Researchers tell us that many students lose points because they give up before they've worked their way through the eight strategies above. Testwise students keep moving along, rapid-fire, ticking off each question in turn—watching for the words that count, looking for tricks, guessing at proba-ble answers as they read the stem, searching quickly among the choices for the answer they prefer, systematically elimi-nating unlikely answers so that they can make an educated guess from the others. They make a stab at each question and move on. They know that the odds are in their favor if they just keep going.

6

True-False Exam Strategies

True-false questions trap the sorts of students who find deeper meanings in everything they read and analyze every problem they encounter. If you have that kind of mind, make yourself work quickly; don't give yourself the luxury of pausing to analyze.

In general, true-false questions test your recognition, not your recall. And they concentrate on facts and details—mostly simple facts and minor details.

STRATEGY 1: READ CAREFULLY

Read every word. Each one is included for a reason, even if it's only to throw you off the track. If you find a phrase that doesn't seem to belong, figure out *why* the test-maker threw it in.

Break down every complex sentence into smaller phrases or sentences that state every one of the thoughts in the longer statement. Each thought has to be true, without exception, or the entire statement is false.

STRATEGY 2: WATCH FOR CLUE WORDS

Look for those little words that can turn an otherwise true statement into one that is false, or vice versa. Researchers have found that statements containing certain words, such as the following, are generally false:

- all
- only
- always
- because

Statements containing certain other words, such as those below, are generally true:

- none
- generally
- usually

STRATEGY 3: DON'T QUIBBLE

Keep in mind that a true statement may be only *approximately* true. Don't quibble. Remember, you are not the one who's going to grade the test. So if you think you have an interpretation of the question that the test-preparer didn't have in mind, forget it! True-false tests are a good place to practice conformity.

Watch out for deliberate traps, but don't search for hidden meanings. Most true-false statements are straightforward and based on key words or phrases you have encountered in the textbook or lectures.

On the other hand, if you feel there *is* a poorly worded statement that could be right or wrong depending on point of view, explain your choice on the answer sheet if it's a hand-scored test. If it's machine-scored, talk to your teacher about the question before you get your grade back.

STRATEGY 4: GUESS

If you don't know an answer, always guess—unless the scoring formula is "rights minus wrongs." In that case, *never* guess.

Hint: There are usually more trues than falses on a test; they are easier to write. In fact, most true sentences come right out of a textbook or a lecture, so if a statement looks familiar, play your hunch.

STRATEGY 5: DON'T CHANGE ANSWERS

In true-false tests, your first hunch is usually correct. So don't change an answer unless you are very sure of the change.

7

Matching Questions Strategies

Few standardized tests include matching questions, but teachers often like them. Students who aren't floored by the sheer length of the lists they are given to match find it easy to pick up extra points by following these strategies.

STRATEGY 1: READ THE DIRECTIONS

Read all directions carefully. Find out whether you are supposed to use each answer only once or any number of times. Keep that in mind as you work.

STRATEGY 2: FIND OUT WHICH COLUMN HAS THE LONGEST PHRASES

Run your eye down both of the columns you have to match. Figure out which one has the *longest* phrases, in general. You'll save time by working your way down *that* column, which means you'll be rereading terms in the column with the shortest entries.

STRATEGY 3: DO THE EASY MATCHES FIRST

Work your way down one column, matching just the ones you know immediately. Especially if each answer can be used just once, match only the ones you are sure of the first time through. Otherwise, if you have to change any of them later, you may be forced to change a bunch all at once. Even on tests that let you use answers more than once, draw a light pencil line through each choice you use.

STRATEGY 4: DO THE TOUGHER MATCHES NEXT

After your first run-through, go back and figure out answers for the ones you aren't so sure of. Look for clues that give away the right answers. Try to find relationships between words in one column and those in the other. For example, while trying to match the name of a group in one column, you may find a synonym for part of its name in the other column: "*Securities* and Exchange Commission" in column A; "*stock* market overseer" in column B. (For other specific clue techniques, turn back to strategies 2 through 7, Chapter 5.)

On the stumpers, try to visualize where in your notes you may have seen those phrases. That alone might help you rule out or single out certain possible matches.

If each phrase can only be used once, you can confine your search to the matches you haven't used yet. But even in multiple-use tests, give first priority to the unused choices; if they don't seem to make a match, then consider the choices you have already used.

8

Verbal Analogy Strategies

Verbal analogies are those sophisticated word problems (cat: dog = seed: _____) found in SATs and other standardized tests. Typically, you are given two words that are somehow related and then told to pick out two other words that are related in the same way. These tests rarely contribute to your grades in courses, but they do determine the courses or schools to which you are admitted.

STRATEGY 1: PRACTICE

The best way to become good at doing verbal analogies is to practice. Find copies of similar tests from earlier years that you can work on (if the answers are available). Or work with a book like the one listed in Appendix A.

It's tough to cram for verbal analogy tests. The best results come from practicing for an hour a day for several weeks before the exam. In fact, several *months* is none too long.

49

STRATEGY 2: GIVE THE EXACT ANSWER CALLED FOR

It doesn't matter what relationships *you* see between words; what counts is what relationship the test-maker sees. Often, the tester's relationship is not as sophisticated as the one you might come up with.

Example: *bigotry: hatred*
(a) sweetness: bitterness
(b) segregation: integration
(c) equality: government
(d) fanaticism: intolerance

If your first conclusion is, "Bigots hate," you probably end up trying to choose between (c) and (d) since people often equate government with equality and fanatics with intolerance. The trouble with such reasoning is that it's highly subjective; many people don't believe that bigots hate, that governments foster equality, or that fanatics are intolerant.

In the above example, you might instead notice that both bigotry and hatred are forms of social excess or extreme, and thus narrow down your choices to (b) and (d) since both are considered social extremes by many people. However, in (b) the related words are *opposites;* in the stem, the words are *not opposites*. If you choose (d) as the correct answer, you're right.

STRATEGY 3: TURN THE ANALOGIES INTO SENTENCES

Read the analogy problems as sentences even if they aren't actually written that way. In the example given above, read, "Bigotry relates to hatred in the same way that sweetness relates to bitterness? segregation relates to integration?

equality relates to government? fanaticism relates to intolerance?"

STRATEGY 4: FIND A WORD FOR THE POSSIBLE RELATIONSHIP

You can work faster and more accurately if you pick out a word—or, at times, two or three words—that describes the relationship between the given analogy words. Here are some of the main relationships.

Purpose: A is used for *B* the same way *X* is used for *Y.*

Cause and effect: A has an effect on *B* the same way *X* has an effect on *Y.*

Part to whole (or individual to group): *A* is part of *B* the same way *X* is part of *Y.*

Part to part: A and *B* are both parts of something the way that *X* and *Y* are both parts of something.

Action to object: A is done to *B* the same way *X* is done to *Y.*

Object to action: A does something to *B* just as *X* does something to *Y.*

Word meaning: A means about the same as *B,* and *X* means about the same as *Y.*

Opposite word meaning: A means about the opposite of *B,* and *X* means about the opposite of *Y.*

Sequence: A comes before (or after) *B* just as *X* comes before (or after) *Y.*

Place: A and *B* are related places just as *X* and *Y* are related places.

Magnitude: A is greater than (or less than) *B* and *X* is greater than (or less than) *Y.*

Grammatical: A and *B* are parts of speech related to each other—noun to noun, adjective to noun, etc.—in the same way that parts of speech *X* and *Y* are related to each other.

Numerical: A is numerically related to B in the same way X is related to Y.

Characteristic: The attributes of A and B are related in the same way as those of X and Y.

STRATEGY 5: ATTACK TOUGH PROBLEMS SYSTEMATICALLY

If you can't figure out a relationship by looking at the first word and then the second, turn them around. See how the second relates to the first. If you still can't come up with a relationship, look for links between the first word of the given analogy and the first word of each answer. Then look for relationships between the second word of the given analogy and the second word of each answer. By that time the correct answer may become very clear.

STRATEGY 6: MAKE EDUCATED GUESSES

As a last resort, eliminate the unlikely answers. For example, if the given analogies are both nouns, you can cross out choices that include a noun and a verb. From the remaining options, let your hunches lead you to a possible right answer.

Since standardized tests are generally organized from easy to tough, if you're near the beginning of an analogy section, think about checking off the least complicated relationship. But, if you're near the end of a particular section, maybe you should mark the most complicated relationship.

If all else fails, if answer (b) hasn't been chosen for a while on your answer sheet, (b) might be a worthwhile choice.

9

Short-Answer and Fill-in-the-Blank Test Strategies

You may never see a fill-in-the-blank question on a standardized test, but many teachers are very fond of them. They test your recall of specific facts—often trivia—and the best way to prepare for them is to memorize thoroughly. Guidelines for preparation appear in Chapter 1 of this book and are developed in much greater detail in *Study Smarts*.

Sometimes fill-in-the-blank questions ask you to supply one word or a short phrase. Occasionally, you have to write down a complete sentence or two. The latter is common when the directions say something like "Define . . ." or "Define and tell the significance of the following." (See Chapter 15 for more on this type of question.)

STRATEGY 1: LOOK FOR CLUES

The language and sentence construction of this kind of test problem very often contain clues about the answer that is expected. If one particular word or phrase is used instead of a more commonly used expression, consider *why* the test-maker did that. If a seemingly unneeded fact is inserted, figure out *why*.

STRATEGY 2: DON'T LOOK TOO HARD FOR HIDDEN MEANING

Remember that short-answer and fill-in-the-blank tests are not very sophisticated. They usually expect little more than accurate recall of key words and phrases used in lectures or readings. So don't think too hard about what's meant by the questions. Don't look for hidden significance that may not be there.

If you've prepared for the test, you will probably do best if you work at a quick pace: read the statement, recall the key words, jot them down, and move on. If you have time at the end of the test, you can go back and reexamine the statements more closely.

STRATEGY 3: WATCH THE BLANKS

Check the number and length of the blanks you have to fill in. Many teachers deliberately let you know whether they expect one word, two words, or three. They may use long blanks when they are looking for long answers and short blanks for short answers. But don't count on it. If you're sure you have come up with the right one-word answer to a two-blank question, put down one word and move on.

STRATEGY 4: OVERANSWER

If you think there may be two answers, put down both of them. Since these tests are always corrected by a person rather than a machine, you should get at least partial credit for your creative answer. Besides, there may be two entirely correct answers, and you might get extra credit for putting them both down.

STRATEGY 5: MAKE EDUCATED GUESSES

If you don't know the specific answer, take an intelligent stab at it. Make up a general answer that uses as much specific information as you can remember. Hedge, if you have to, with words such as *tends to, may, often;* that way, your answer may get at least partial credit from a benevolent grader.

Educated guessing often turns out to be a lot more than just a shot in the dark. Your subconscious probably remembers more key words from the textbook than you would expect. Let your fingers start to fill in some of the blanks that have you stumped, and see how often the right answer flows onto the paper.

10

Vocabulary Test Strategies

Vocabulary problems are a favorite on standardized tests. Your knowledge of the English language is supposed to demonstrate how much you have learned in school and generally how intelligent you are. On these tests, being testwise can give you a great advantage. A few points on a vocabulary test can make the difference between getting or losing a scholarship you've had your eye on or between being accepted and rejected for the career program you want to get into. Therefore, the following strategies may pay larger dividends than anything else in your entire school career.

STRATEGY 1: WHEN YOU KNOW THE WORD, WATCH OUT FOR TRAPS

Traps are considered part of the game in testing circles. They even have a pretty name: *attractive distractors*. We have found an actual sample vocabulary test question that is all traps. We'll analyze it so you can see how to avoid such traps when you run into them.

Example: Find a close synonym for the word *coalescence:*
(a) fusion   (b) fission   (c) fissure   (d) unite   (e) coal

Tactic 1: Beware of words similar to the right answer

The right answer in our example is *fusion.* But *fission* was inserted because it looks like *fusion,* and many people confuse fusion with fission. Not content with that trick, the test-designer also stuck in *fissure,* perhaps to trick testwise students who were confused by fusion/fission. (In multiple-choice questions, the real answer is very often camouflaged with a wrong answer that looks or sounds similar to it.)

Tactic 2: Watch out for words that sound like the stem

Often a word is stuck in that looks like or sounds like the stem (the word you have to define). *Coal* is that kind of trap in our example above.

Tactic 3: Watch for grammar

Often a possible answer is wrong only because it's the wrong part of speech. *Unite,* in our example, is just that kind of trap. *Unite* is a verb; *coalescence* is a noun. And that's *all* that makes answer (d) incorrect. If the stem word were *coalesce* (a verb), then *unite* would be correct and *fusion* wrong.

STRATEGY 2: IF THE WORD SEEMS FAMILIAR, THINK

Very often the stem word seems vaguely familiar, but you can't put your finger on exactly what it means. In that case, it's a good idea to jog your memory before you try to pick out the right answer through mere elimination. Try the following tricks.

- If you have ever used the word, try to remember how.
- Try to remember where you've seen or heard the word used.
- Try to use it in a sentence that makes sense. Then substitute each option in the same sentence. The ones that don't make sense probably are not right choices.
- Change the word stem into other parts of speech that you may be able to recognize more easily.

At the very least, going through these steps—quickly—will help you pull out everything you know about the word. Then pick the answer that feels correct. Remember, it's rare for two words to mean *exactly* the same thing; look for words that have *most nearly* the same meaning.

STRATEGY 3: IF YOU DON'T KNOW THE WORD, MAKE AN EDUCATED GUESS

Here's how to make your educated guesses pay off as frequently as possible, when you don't know a word at all.

Tactic 1: Try association

Associate the word, or parts of it, with words you already know. For example, if you're stuck on *fusion* in our example above, maybe you can recall that *fuse* means to *come together* or that the wire in an electrical fuse *melts together* into a ball.

Tactic 2: Eliminate wrong parts of speech

Cross out any answers that are given in the wrong part of

speech. Even if you don't know a word's meaning, you probably have a pretty sound notion about whether it's a noun, a verb, or an adjective.

If you aren't sure whether or not a word is a verb, put *to* in front of it; if it sounds all right, it is probably a verb. (Example: *to coalescence* sounds funny. It's not a verb.) If you are unsure whether or not a word is a noun, put *the* in front of it; if it sounds OK, it's probably a noun. (Example: *the coalescence* sounds OK. It is a noun.)

Tactic 3: Rule out stem word look-alikes

If you have to guess blindly, eliminate answers that look or sound like the stem word. Most of them are traps.

Tactic 4: Watch out for answer look-alikes

If two answers look or sound alike, you can be pretty sure they contain some kind of clue. If you're still in the easy part of the test (the earlier part of most standardized test sections), one of the two words is probably the right answer. But if you're in the difficult section, the odds are high that both words are part of a trick—the same kind of trick we saw in the above example in which both *fission* and *fissure* were wrong answers.

Tactic 5: Don't leave any blanks

Leave a problem unanswered only if (1) the number of wrong answers is deducted from the number of right answers, *and* (2) you can't narrow down the answers to three (or fewer) logical choices. Otherwise the odds are usually in your favor if you make an educated guess.

STRATEGY 4: IF YOU KNOW A SECOND LANGUAGE, USE IT

If you can speak or read a language other than English, use it to find clues on vocabulary tests. English is derived from many different languages: Latin, Italian, French, German, and others. Often the other language you know will help you make sense out of unfamiliar English words.

Whether or not you speak a second language, it pays to memorize common English suffixes, roots, and prefixes. We have listed many of them in Appendix D.

STRATEGY 5: PRACTICE

You can learn how to take vocabulary tests like a whiz. Invest in some practice books and then practice the strategies until you can use them all quickly and automatically. Most vocabulary tests are time tests, so work against the clock.

11

Number Problem Strategies

You can count on getting better test scores if you attack number problems correctly. It doesn't matter whether the course is math, engineering, or science. It doesn't matter whether it's a standardized test or a teacher-prepared quiz.

STRATEGY 1: WORK SYSTEMATICALLY

Try to find out in advance whether simple arithmetic errors count and, if they do, how much they count. If knowing the correct method for solving the problem is worth 90 percent, and finding the right answer is worth only 10 percent, don't spend much more than 10 percent of your time on the arithmetic. Don't even double-check your numbers unless you have plenty of time left at the end of the test.

On the other hand, if your answer has to be exact, your working habits should be exact, too. Researchers have found out that one out of every five wrong answers on math tests is caused by carelessness or mistakes made in working with simple numbers. Here's how to work accurately.

Tactic 1: Write carefully

Learn to write your numbers carefully so that even under pressure your sevens don't look like ones or fours, and your eights don't look like sixes or zeros. Many students make a European seven (7) to protect against mistakes.

Tactic 2: Write in columns

For simple arithmetic or elaborate calculations, keep all digits in line; it improves your accuracy, and it helps when you go back to check your work later. There's a reason why your third-grade teacher made you learn to write neat columns for adding and subtracting—it makes a difference.

Tactic 3: Copy accurately

If you have to copy a problem onto work paper, check to make absolutely sure you've copied *all* the numbers and copied them *all* correctly. If you have time at the end of the test, check once more. You'd be surprised at how often you can't discover a dumb mistake—such as reading "8" but writing "6"—until the pressure is off.

Tactic 4: Watch for units of measure

Before you start working on a problem, deliberately stop and check the units of measurement. This is a major source of wrong answers. If some of the given numbers are not in the proper units of measurement, change them. Be sure that you know and understand what units the answer is supposed to be given in.

Tactic 5: Don't play hero

If you are allowed to use a calculator, use one. But check your answers anyway. It's as easy to punch in the wrong number as it is to write down the wrong number. The best way to check an answer is to work backward, starting with your answer and finding one of the givens.

STRATEGY 2: ORGANIZE YOUR WORK

Before you start working on a problem, organize all parts of it systematically and deliberately. Actually write down:

- the given numbers;
- what you are supposed to find;
- all formulas you're going to need, listed in the order in which you expect to use them.

If you're taking a classroom test, write all this down on your answer sheet. For a machine-scored test that you're not supposed to mark up, use scrap paper or write lightly on the question sheet and erase when you are finished. On some tests, you'll be able to circle or underline the *givens* and the *find,* which means you will just have to jot down the necessary formulas.

STRATEGY 3: USE GRAPHICS

If you find a particular problem complicated, draw a diagram, graph, sketch—anything that will help you make better sense of the problem. Label the *givens* on all your diagrams.

STRATEGY 4: ESTIMATE

If you can, estimate the answer before you start to work

out the solution. This is a fast check on whether or not you have used the right method and written the numbers accurately. It's also a check on whether or not you have read your calculator accurately.

Example: *Given a tank 2.2 feet in diameter and filled to 6.5 feet, what is the maximum weight of the water in the tank?*

First, jot down the givens as well as the formula ($V = \pi r^2 h$) and the weight of water at 4°C. = 62.43 lb./cu. ft. Then estimate by using $r = 1$, $h = 6$, $\pi = 3$, and water's weight = 60. So $1 \times 3 = 3$; $3 \times 6 = 18$; round that to 20; and $20 \times 60 = 1{,}200$. The actual answer comes out to 1,541.8, so if you get 154.2 or 15,418, suspect a misplaced decimal point. If you get 6,167.11, you will know your error is more complicated. (You would eventually discover that you forgot to divide the 2.2-foot diameter by 2 to find the 1.1-foot radius.)

STRATEGY 5: USE ALL THE INFORMATION

Make sure that your calculations use all the information given in the problem. If you feel that some data is really extraneous, think about it. It's a rare math problem that tricks you by providing too many facts or figures.

STRATEGY 6: STUDY GRAPHS CAREFULLY

If the problem incorporates a graph or similar illustration, study it as well as all of its labels. Here are some things to watch for on graphs:

- Do the *X* and *Y* axis values begin at zero?
- Do the values extend linearly or do they skip to save space?
- Are the values linear? Logarithmic?
- Are the graph's units identical to units of the givens in the rest of the problem?

STRATEGY 7: REREAD THE QUESTION

After you have found what you hope is the right answer, reread the question.

- If you're required to show your work, have you done so?
- Did you answer in the correct units?
- Did you answer all parts of the question?
- Does your understanding of the problem on *second* reading agree with your first reading?

STRATEGY 8: DON'T QUIT

If you're stuck on a problem, try substituting rounded-off numbers for fractions, or real numbers for algebraic symbols. Sometimes, if you pause to think through the problem in its simplest form, it will be just a short jump to solving the problem in its more complicated form.

If you have absolutely no idea of how to do the problem, figure out what information you're missing. Can you find it in some other problem? Do you know how to derive the missing formula or even approximate it? Are you really missing something or just not reading well?

STRATEGY 9: ATTACK MULTIPLE-CHOICE NUMBER QUESTIONS SYSTEMATICALLY

Testwise students have a system for solving multiple-choice number problems as quickly and accurately as possible.

Tactic 1: Don't look at the answers

Solve the problem before you look at the choices. Work it

out on paper if you have to, in your head if you're sure of yourself. Then look for your answer among the choices. If it isn't there, you know you've done something wrong—unless you have some of those oddball choices such as "none of the above" or "not enough information to decide."

Tactic 2: Estimate

If speed is important, just estimate the answer. On a great many multiple-choice speed tests, the test-maker is simply checking your knowledge of the right formulas and methods. When that's the case, they usually select answer choices that don't trip up estimators.

Tactic 3: Make educated guesses

Any answer is better than no answer. If you don't know how to solve the problem, make an educated guess. Here's how to go about it.

- Eliminate all answer choices that are given in unlikely measurements.
- You can often eliminate the highest and lowest values among the possible answers.
- From the remaining possibilities, pick the most likely answer.
- Move on quickly to the next problem.

12

Math or Figure Series Test Problems

Some test-takers seem to be born knowing how to whiz through these IQ puzzlers which give you a series of numbers, geometric figures, or letters and tell you to supply a missing part of the series—either at the end or somewhere in the middle. The rest of us have to attack such problems with a system that gets us the maximum number of points.

These tests are nonverbal. They try to measure your ability to reason instead of your ability to work with words. But the same strategies that can help you pick up extra points on word reasoning tests will help you with math or figure series tests.

STRATEGY 1: UNDERSTAND WHAT IS CALLED FOR

Sometimes the directions seem terribly complicated. That's probably because verbal ability is not a requirement for people who prepare these tests. But, almost invariably, what you're supposed to do is: (1) figure out the rule used to create the series of numbers, letters, or shapes, and then (2) use that rule to figure out which number, letter, or shape comes next (or is missing along the way).

When you try to make sense out of the directions on these tests, you'll save time if you *start* by assuming that they follow the general rule we have just given. *Then* read carefully to make sure that they do not *deviate* from the rule.

STRATEGY 2: GUESS FIRST

Since your hunches are usually right when you take tests such as these, take a good guess at the answer first. But check your hunch: plug your choice into the series and make sure that the rule carries through. If you have to supply a missing number (or other part) in the middle of a series, don't just test whether or not the rule applies from the beginning *to* your choice; also keep going from your choice to *the end*.

STRATEGY 3: LOOK FOR SIMPLE PATTERNS

In number series, the relationship or pattern you must find generally will be one of these:

- addition
- subtraction
- multiplication
- division
- squaring
- cubing
- taking square root
- taking cube root (occasionally)

To complicate your life, some series use more than one of

these operations at a time. For example, this series uses two rules:

$$1 \quad 4 \quad 25 \quad 676 \quad \underline{\hspace{1.5cm}}$$

In studying the series, you should notice right away that the numbers increase very quickly; they increase *almost* geometrically. That should be a clue that the rule probably involves squaring or cubing. But 1 squared or cubed is still 1. So you would have to start figuring out what rule was used in addition to squaring. *Add* 1 to 1 and then *square* the 2; that results in 4. But don't stop there. See what you get if you add 1 to 4 and then square the 5. Right! You get 25. Add 1 again, square again, and you get 676. So that's the rule. All you have to do next is add 1 to 676 and square the 677, giving the correct answer of 458,329.

The same rule applies to letter series: look for simple arithmetic patterns. Look at this example:

$$c \quad f \quad i \quad l \quad o \quad r \quad \underline{\hspace{1.5cm}}$$

If these were numbers instead of letters, you would have the answer in a second. Don't let the letters throw you. Run down the list of simple math procedures: addition, subtraction, multiplication, division. Here you'll stop at addition, since the letters progress by threes. The next letter should be *u.*

STRATEGY 4: LOOK FOR SUBPATTERNS AND SUBGROUPINGS

If you've found a pattern that works for all but a few numbers or letters, start looking for subgroupings that, taken as units, follow another rule. The following is an example:

$$2 \quad 5 \quad 11 \quad 22 \quad 45 \quad 91 \quad \underline{\hspace{1cm}} \quad 205$$

To get 5 and 11, you double the previous number and add 1. To get 45 and 91 you double the previous number and add 1. But 22 and the missing number break that pattern, so you must look for a second pattern to add to the first one.

An average student might look for a relationship between 2 and 22 and search the answer choices for 222 or 42 (one or both of which may be there to stump the unwary). But the testwise student knows that 205 is the first clue to use. Reversing the first rule and working backward, you come up with 102. Then you plug it into the series to check it against the second pattern: 2 5 11 22 45 91 102 205. It's obvious that 102 doesn't relate to 22 in the same way 22 does to 2, but 102 does relate to 91 the same way 22 relates to its predecessor, 11. So you can be sure that answer is correct.

If you can analyze patterns that are this complex, you can conquer most series tests with ease.

To isolate groupings, follow visual clues. Here's an actual exam question:

$$b \quad a \quad k \quad r \quad m \quad v \quad m \quad v \quad k \quad r \quad \underline{\hspace{1cm}}$$

Notice how letters start repeating after *m v.* They go back to *m v,* then repeat the adjacent *pair* of letters, *k r.* Next must come the remaining pair, *b a,* so the correct answer for this series is *b.*

STRATEGY 5: USE THE MULTIPLE-CHOICE PROBLEM CLUES

Most math or figure series problems use multiple-choice

formats. In these cases, clues are even easier to find. If you can't immediately locate the pattern or patterns that form the rule, you can run through a quick elimination to test which of the four or five choices steers you to the rule or rules. But do double-check, as we pointed out in Strategy 4. (For additional help, reread Chapter 5 on how to work with multiple-choice tests.)

STRATEGY 6: PRACTICE

Plenty of old exams and practice books are available that will give you practice solving math series problems. Invest in them and test yourself against the clock, since most of these are time tests.

13

Reading Comprehension Test Strategies

You won't find reading comprehension problems on teacher-prepared exams because they don't test whether or not you have learned anything in a course. They're supposed to gauge whether you can *find* or *figure out* information contained in a given reading passage, and are popular in standardized tests. As with every other test, the testwise student has a decided edge.

STRATEGY 1: IGNORE THE INSTRUCTIONS

Most instructions tell you to read the passage and then answer the questions. Don't do it. Read the *questions* first. You'll save lots of time that way. Since most reading comprehension tests are time tests, the more time you save, the more points you can score.

If the questions ask for specific factual material contained in the reading, it seldom pays to read the entire passage carefully. Skim it to find the facts, supply the facts, and move on.

Reading comprehension questions often ask you to make conclusions or draw inferences about what the author is saying in the passage. To supply such nonspecific information, you will have to read the entire passage. But if you've read the questions first, you'll have a better idea of what you are reading for.

STRATEGY 2: USE YOUR TIME WISELY

Reading comprehension tests are usually time tests. So plan to use your time to answer as many of the easiest questions as possible.

Tactic 1: Don't skip around after reading passages

If one passage looks difficult after you read it, don't skip to the next one and plan to come back later. Reading selections are almost always arranged with the easier ones first, the more difficult ones last. Skipping around *after* you've read the passages can only waste time.

Tactic 2: Locate the easiest questions

If you are good at finding factual references in the reading passages, but poor at forming conclusions, do the factual passages first. As you read the questions, which you should do before reading the passages, if you find "conclusions" questions, mark them and go on to skim the next set of questions.

STRATEGY 3: CHECK YOUR ANSWERS

After you have chosen an answer, compare it to the sentence that gave you the answer:

- Be sure that the answer covers *all parts* of the question.

- Be sure that you have checked the answer you intended to check; students lose too many points by *finding* the correct answer but *checking* the wrong one.

STRATEGY 4: DON'T ADD ANY FACTS

Base your answers entirely on facts contained in the reading passage. Even if you know something about the subject, remember that this is a test of your ability to read and understand *a given passage*. Applying your outside knowledge can only cost you points, unless the instructions specifically tell you to apply it.

STRATEGY 5: FORGET YOUR OWN CONCLUSIONS

Keep reminding yourself that you're being tested on your understanding of the words, sentences, facts, and ideas *in the passage*—nothing more unless specifically asked for. If you think the author's facts or conclusions are wrong, keep that to yourself; answer questions based on the author's facts and the author's conclusions, and only those. Especially if you know something about the subject, read carefully; students lose points because they jump to conclusions based on their own preconceptions. Be sure that you can point to the reading passage that supports the conclusions reached in the answer you want to mark.

14

Essay Exam Strategies

Many people think that essay exams are the least biased in favor of testwise students. But the truth is that testwise students can rack up extra points on essay exams as easily as they can on any other kind of test.

First, prepare for every essay exam. We included several strategies for that in Chapter 1. Then, during the exam, get organized. You can raise your score significantly if you organize your answers and work efficiently. Ironically, the most efficient way to answer essay questions is not to grab your pen and write nonstop. Here are the strategies that have worked for naturally testwise students; they will also work for you.

STRATEGY 1: FIND OUT WHO IS GRADING THE ESSAYS

It pays to take into account who will be marking your essay exam. If it's your teacher or teaching assistant, you'll know what kind of answers the individual likes; for example, lots of details, lots of philosophical interpretations, lots of new outlooks on old topics, or simply rewrites of everything you've had in lectures.

On the other hand, if a stranger is going to be reading your essay exam, don't take chances. Don't spout unpopular viewpoints. Don't start to reinterpret basic aspects of the subject. Don't skimp on specific facts. The more facts you include, the more people assume you know about a subject.

STRATEGY 2: READ ALL THE QUESTIONS

Before you begin to answer any essay question, read them all. Take a minute or two to list what you know about each question. Use one word or a short phrase for each and jot down all the relevant facts, formulas, names, dates, ideas, and impressions that come to mind. This serves three important functions:

- It gets everything down on paper while you are relaxed. This prevents the horrible situation that sometimes occurs—when you get so involved in the answer for one question that your mind blocks out the information you need for the next question.
- It shows graphically how much you know about each question. That way, if you have to choose which questions to answer—a popular essay test format—you'll be able to choose the ones you know the most about.
- It starts your memory flowing. That way, while you're answering *one* question your mind may be dredging up facts and interpretations for *other* questions. If that happens, by the way, be sure to jot down the new information on your list; otherwise you may forget about it later on or have to work so hard at remember-

ing it again that you'll have less time to spend on the actual answer.

STRATEGY 3: REREAD THE DIRECTIONS

Go back and read the directions one more time. Make sure you understand them. Underline or jot down key words so you can refer back to them quickly. We'd underline: *use both sides of the paper; choose one from section A and two from section B; cite at least three major researchers.*

It's a good idea to reread the directions before you start each new question. There's no sense in losing points for failure to follow simple instructions.

STRATEGY 4: BUDGET YOUR TIME

If all questions are worth the same number of points, divide your time equally among all the answers. (If some questions are worth more than others, keep *that* in mind as you budget your time.) Then, divide up your time for each answer so that you spend 50 percent of it *outlining* your answer and 50 percent *writing*.

This advice may sound strange at first, but it's really the key to higher marks. Researchers have found that essay exam graders—even those trained by the College Board to correct SAT essays—give most credit for *content,* second most credit for *organization.* Content and organization together account for most of your essay's grade. Spelling, grammar, and mechanics usually make up a very small part of your overall test grade, though a few English teachers count them a great deal.

A good outline is the key to getting all your content down on paper and to getting it there as well organized as possible. It's also the fastest and most accurate way of working. That's why we advise you to spend half your time on every question outlining your answer.

STRATEGY 5: REREAD EVERY QUESTION CAREFULLY

You should read questions on essay exams every bit as carefully as you read math problems. Label, underline, or jot down everything that's *given*. Do the same for *what* you're supposed to cover, as well as *how* you are supposed to answer.

Some essay tests, especially the standardized ones, have paragraphs of given information. They generally expect you to work the givens into your essay; be sure you don't overlook any of them.

Here's an example adapted from a College Board essay exam:

> Wastefulness is part of the American way of life. We use three packages or wrappings when one would do, build machines to be obsolete in five years, and generally waste time, energy, and natural resources. Yet we consider thrift a virtue, and we consider ourselves efficient.
>
> Are these statements justified? Do they tell us anything about ourselves? Explain and defend your answer, using illustrations from your reading, study, and observation.

Here are the notes we would jot down for such an essay:

Given: wastefulness—three wraps, not one
                —machines obsolete in five years

    waste—time
        —energy
        —natural resources

> BUT—consider thrift a virtue
>   ″   ourselves efficient

> Prove: justify or refute (given statements)
>   show if they tell anything about us

> Method: explain/defend
>   use reading, study, observation

STRATEGY 6: PICK A TITLE

Choose a working title for your essay even if the exam doesn't require one. It pays to spend up to a fourth of your alloted time on picking the right title because it will keep you on track and ensure that you answer the right question—as well as the whole question.

Your working title should include:

- the topic
- the approach (or point of view) that you will use
- the boundaries of the assigned topic
- nothing that is off the topic

For the essay used as an example at the end of Strategy 5, a good working title might be: "Efficiency and Thrift: How Americans Preach One Thing but Practice the Opposite."

Poor working titles for the same example are:

- "Americans Preach Efficiency but Practice Waste." (It doesn't include one of the givens: *thrift.*)
- "The Meaning of Thrift and Waste." (It *explains* but doesn't include any *defense,* which is part of the assignment; it also includes *everybody,* not just Americans—another detail stressed in the given.)

STRATEGY 7: OUTLINE YOUR ESSAY

As we said earlier, this can win you the most points. So don't rush through it. Outline time is time well spent.

Tactic 1: Jot down the content

You will probably be able to rework notes you made at the time you read each essay question. But make sure to start thinking of those notes in terms of a well-argued essay. Here's what you are going to need:

(1) General statements: the major conclusions you are expected to prove, disprove, agree with, disagree with, and so forth. They can be your own opinions (except in most scientific essays), but you'll be safer to adopt statements made by the test-giver. The safest approach of all is to restate all the major statements contained in the givens.

(2) Evidence that supports each general statement. If time and space allow, shoot for three pieces of evidence to support each general statement. If you have fewer, your argument may sound thin and undocumented; more can sound superfluous. Each fact must tie in clearly to the general statement it is supposed to support. A fact that mentions its source is better than an unattributed fact. But concrete facts—even without sources—are better than fuzzy opinions.

In the previous example of an essay question (shown at the end of Strategy 5), three general statements and several pieces of possible evidence were suggested by the question itself. We would jot them down this way:

    1. Wastefulness is part of American way of life.
      a. Three packages when one would do.
      b. Build machines obsolete in five years.
      c. Waste time, energy, resources (generally).
        (Find more specific examples.)

2. Americans consider thrift a virtue.
   a.
   b.
   c.
3. We consider ourselves efficient.
   a.
   b.
   c.
4. Conclusion: Why don't we preach what we practice?

Once you have filled in some specific factual evidence to back up the general statements, you're ready to move on to the next step.

Tactic 2: Estimate how many words you have to write

It will help you use your time most efficiently, and ensure that you'll offer as much evidence as possible, if you plan to write as many pages as you can handle. Here's a chart that will help you budget your time and guess at how much evidence the test-grader expects from you.

Time allotted per essay question	Total words expected per essay question	Number of details given for each major point
2 to 5 minutes	20 to 30 words	none
10 to 15 minutes	50 to 75 words	1 for each
20 to 30 minutes	100 to 150 words	2 for each
45 to 60 minutes	300 to 500 words	3 for each

Tactic 3: Organize your outline

Use the list from Tactic 1 and the guidelines from Tactic 2 to help you organize the final form of your outline. The order in which you jotted down the notes is probably not the most logical way to present them in your essay. Remember, if you don't take the time to organize your topics logically you can lose valuable points.

Certain kinds of information suggest obvious methods of organization. Reports of events should be organized chronologically. Directions or reports on experiments should be presented in the same order in which you or some researcher did them. Descriptions of people, places, and things should be organized according to how the eye might see them, moving from a general overview to a description of each specific important part in turn.

Since most essays deal not with *events* but with *ideas,* you may have trouble finding the correct organization. If this is a common problem for you, let Appendix C be your guide. We have listed there all the common ways of organizing even the toughest essays.

In general, you can chalk up the highest number of possible points on essays about ideas if you put your strongest points first. It pays to show the test-grader right at the beginning how well you can recall facts and how logically you can tackle a difficult subject. You will immediately sound like an A student, and your essay will be read like an A student's exam.

No matter what kind of logical organization you start with, stick with it. If you change methods of organization halfway through your essay, you are likely to lose points.

STRATEGY 8: GET INVOLVED IN YOUR ESSAY

If you can whip up some enthusiasm in your essay, you'll probably get a better grade. Your essay will be more enjoyable to read if you show some emotional involvement or concern. Your essay will also seem much more convincing and therefore much stronger and much better reasoned. And if you are interested in what you're writing, you will improve the content and organization.

On the other hand, don't write a tirade. And don't forget that your emotions are supposed to be influenced by the facts you are presenting, not the other way around. You are, after all, writing an essay exam for a professor, not an advice for the lovelorn column.

STRATEGY 9: WRITE METHODICALLY

A good essay test answer should be almost as well written as a good term paper. And it should have all the same elements: title, topic statement, standard organization, and ending. (If you need more than a quick review of these, or you want some help with writing in general, we suggest you locate a copy of our companion book *Secrets to Writing Great Papers* (University of Wisconsin Press, 2003).

Tactic 1: Write a topic statement

The finest way to write a topic statement is simply to rework your title into a complete sentence. Example: "When it comes to efficiency and thrift, Americans preach one thing but practice another." Then, on longer essays, summarize the general statements you plan to make by using the very same phrases you jotted down in your outline.

There are two reasons for going through this elaborate opening. First, it makes you seem very well organized—and that's worth points. Next, it alerts the reader to watch for the major topics that you plan to cover, and, if your handwriting is horrible, *that* can also be worth points. (If you say that you are going to talk about something, and you don't do so, the grader may not even notice that if your handwriting is *really* horrible.)

Tactic 2: Organize your body

In general, you should devote one paragraph to each of the general statements of your outline. If it's not a broad enough topic to be worth a whole paragraph, it's probably not important enough to consider in a generalization.

Start each paragraph with the general statement, written in a good English sentence. Then tell about each piece of evidence in turn. Be sure that you tie the evidence clearly to the statement it's supposed to prove.

Skip a line between paragraphs (unless test instructions tell you not to do so). This makes your paper easier to read, and it allows room for you to add an extra point if you think of one later. Don't skip *two* lines, however, or the test-maker may think you're short of information.

Tactic 3: Write long

This is an art that many testwise students master at an early age. They write down lots of details, lots of specifics, lots of examples, lots of sources of information. It takes a little extra time, but if the reader is trying to decide between grades of A and B, it will be worth the extra time.

If you know a topic cold, it can be fun to show off. But be sure that everything you write down applies to the topic. You may gain a point or two for knowing so many facts, but you could also lose five or ten points for not knowing how to organize your essay.

If time permits, consider opposing viewpoints and add some novel interpretations of your own. They generally result in a few extra points. But first make sure that you've got the original viewpoint and the standard interpretations explained *solidly* and backed up with three documented facts at every point along the way. Then, clearly label your extra-credit writing as your own interpretation of the data or whatever other description is appropriate.

It's time-saving and practical to use clear labeling words throughout your essay. *Example, exceptions, contrasts, comparisons, evidence, supports, arguments,* and *counterarguments* are good labeling words. You might even underline them. They alert the harried reader that you're about to say something crucial or that you are about to shift gears.

If you get writer's block—don't know quite how to write something so that it's clear or clever—sit back and imagine yourself saying it to someone. Then write it that way. Don't get hung up looking for just the right phrase. If you have time later, you can go back and smooth out the trouble spot. If not, it's more important that you put down all the important information. Remember, content and organization count for most of your score.

STRATEGY 10: WRITE AN ENDING

It's important to tie your essay together at the end. It helps you check whether or not you have covered the topic thoroughly, and it shows the grader one last time how well organized and thorough you've been throughout the essay.

A sentence or two is ending enough. There are two easy ways to end:

- Summarize the general points you have made. Be sure, however, that you don't throw in anything new. This is a shortcoming of many essay writers. They get to the end of their essay's body, relax a bit, and remember something entirely new and exciting. So they tack it onto the end of the essay. Instead of exciting the test-maker, this ending generally turns on the red ink— because it looks like you didn't take time to develop that last thought.

- Restate your topic sentence. Example: "It looks like Americans will have to keep on preaching thrift but practicing waste, since that's what keeps the capitalist system going."

STRATEGY 11: CHECK YOUR WORK

After you have finished the exam, if there's time left over, reread each question and the essay that goes with it. Be sure that you have answered all that was asked for—and only what was asked for.

Tactic 1: Check for content

- Have you stuck to your original point of view or changed somewhere along the way?
- Have you proven each argument with enough specific facts?
- Have you clearly separated facts from opinions and labeled each?
- Have you carefully hedged on your general statements by using qualifiers such as *most* and *probably* whenever you couldn't prove that a statement is always true?
- Have you mentioned the exceptions to your general statements?

Tactic 2: Check for organization

- Did you open with a topic sentence?
- Is the topic sentence too narrow or too broad for the essay that follows?
- What kind of organization did you plan to use in the body of your essay? Did you follow it?
- Did you cover all the points in your original outline?
- Do you have a satisfying ending?

- Does your ending drop any new information that shouldn't be there?

Tactic 3: Check your writing mechanics

- Does every sentence say what you mean it to say?
- Are you sure of the meanings for all the words?
- Is your handwriting legible (where you want it to be)? (If you're forced to hedge or fudge on a fact here and there, that's where your handwriting can go bad. Everywhere else, the test-reader should have a fighting chance to read what you wrote.)
- Are spelling, grammar, punctuation, and sentence structure all right? They are sometimes important in English and journalism courses. Otherwise they count for very little. Work on them only if you have plenty of time.

STRATEGY 12: WHAT TO DO IF YOU PREPARED FOR THE WRONG TOPICS

If you studied for all the wrong questions, the worst you can do is get a big zero. With some artful dodging, you might still walk out with an A.

First jot down the questions you are prepared to answer. Compare your questions to the ones on the exam paper. Look for overlap in general subject matter. *Look especially for ambiguously worded questions that overlap the questions you are prepared to answer.* Testwise students know that if they write a well-organized, well-documented, thorough answer that partly misses the point of a question, they will certainly get partial credit. And if the question was ambiguous to begin with, they stand a chance to win full credit.

Since testwise students are doing this right now, and getting credit for doing it, we figure everybody ought to be aware of their methods.

STRATEGY 13: HOW TO STRETCH YOUR INFORMATION

If you discover that you don't have enough facts and other details to support the general statements you have to make on a particular question, there are two ways to stretch out what you do know. There are inherent risks in both methods, but the risk in using no method at all is probably much greater.

First, you can choose, from the facts you *do* know, the ones that most clearly fit into the discussion. Then tie them as artfully as you can to the statement. This will require some reaching and stretching of arguments. You may lose some points for organization while you gain some for content. Either way, you have nothing to lose by trying.

Alternately, you can choose the favorite method of test-wise students who are whizzes at debate. They organize an essay so that the first topics are the ones they know best. For each of those early topics they offer an abundance of details, facts, supports, and examples. Then when they reach the topics in which the going will get rough, they carefully lay out the generalization at the start of a paragraph, and then casually write something like, "But of course, this argument would fall apart as quickly as earlier arguments did after a careful examination of the facts."

This ruse works best on essay exams in which many students have more questions than time. It also works best in the hands of students who walk into the exam room with luck and guts.

STRATEGY 14: WHAT TO DO IF YOU RUN OUT OF TIME

If you find that you've just about run out of time, write

that fact on your paper. Then copy, as neatly and completely as possible, your essay's outline. You stand a good chance of earning at least partial credit, and some teachers give full credit for a well-organized outline that demonstrates a good understanding of the subject's content.

15

Identify-and-Explain Test Strategies

Many teachers are fond of the kind of exam in which you're given a list of words and told to write a sentence or two that sums up everything important about the subject. The following strategies should help you pick up extra credit.

STRATEGY 1: START WITH THE SUBJECT'S NAME

Always start your answer by giving the subject's name. If the list only gives a person's initials, and you can give the complete name (plus title), do so.

STRATEGY 2: USE DESCRIPTIVE WORDS

Immediately after telling the subject's name, describe the subject—whether person or thing—as fully but briefly as you can. Use colorful but specific words whenever possible: an *infamous* general, a *self-serving* commission, a *much-*

maligned corporation. However, if you aren't sure of some detail, pick a word that covers up your lapse of memory; for example, if you aren't sure whether a particular subject is a corporation, a syndicate, or a trade association, *organization* is a safe word to use.

STRATEGY 3: TELL WHEN AND WHERE THE SUBJECT WAS IMPORTANT

It's impressive to be able to tell the period of time when the subject was important. If you are sure of the actual date when he did something noteworthy, give it; if you are not certain about a specific date, try to drop a general phrase into one of your sentences. Here's an example: "During *the early 1920s,* when James Joyce was working on *Ulysses.* . . ." That phrase might disguise the fact that you forgot that the book was published in 1922.

Be sure to tell *where* the subject did whatever it was he did. If you're writing an American History exam, give the name of the colony or the state; for a world history course, give at least the country. Even in a science course, it pays to tell that Curie was French and Jenner was British.

STRATEGY 4: TELL WHY THE PERSON, PLACE, OR THING WAS IMPORTANT

Give at least one reason why the subject was important. Be as specific as you can. Again, if you can't be specific, choose words that cover up your memory lapse. If you're afraid that any part of your answer is too general because you really don't remember as much as you should, try to work into your answer some fact, figure, or date that *is* obviously specific—even if it is not 100 percent on the topic

16

Oral Exam Strategies

Like any other kind of exam, you can prepare for oral exams. And you can become testwise enough to score extra points during your orals.

Since you must be able to speak fluently and clearly, with little time for organizing your thoughts, many oral examiners permit you to choose your topic in advance. Even when you can't, most will at least tell you the scope of the exam— if you ask. Your exam actually begins right then, when you begin your preparation, because a substantial part of your grade will depend on how well you prepare.

STRATEGY 1: ZERO IN ON A TOPIC

It's best to choose a very limited topic and then discuss it in great depth and with many details. If you choose a broad topic, you risk appearing superficial because you will only have time to make sweeping generalizations about it.

Learn how to zero in on a topic that's limited enough in scope that you can cover it with lots of details within the allotted time. (A fifteen-minute speech is approximately equivalent to a four-page essay.) Our earlier discussion of essay exams will help you choose a topic.

STRATEGY 2: THINK IN THREES

Your talk will seem most impressive if it makes three points about the topic and then offers three pieces of specific evidence about each point. So practice thinking in threes.

STRATEGY 3: PUBLIC SPEAKING TAKES PRACTICE

An oral exam is actually a form of public speaking. So you can prepare for your presentation by practicing public speaking. Start early in the semester that ends with an oral exam and join some kind of group that has large meetings or attend town meetings or forums presided over by bigwigs—people whose presence might intimidate you. Force yourself to speak from the audience to such groups on topics that concern you. The more practice you have doing this, the more comfortable you will feel when you walk into your oral exam.

If you have real psychological problems about speaking in front of groups, get counseling for it *before* the exam.

STRATEGY 4: MAKE A GOOD IMPRESSION

Oral exam grades can be quite subjective, so arrive prepared to make a good impression. Dress appropriately. If you aren't sure what to wear, overdress just a bit. Look neat and well scrubbed. Comb your hair.

If you are supposed to stand up to speak, act confident—even if you aren't. Plant your feet firmly and don't fidget or keep moving around. Look over your audience before you start. If there's a podium, lay your notes on it and stand behind it; you can grab it if you need a way to keep your hands from shaking during the first few frightening minutes.

If your voice cracks or sounds funny to you, don't let it throw you; most of the people in the room have probably never heard you speak. They will assume that this is your normal voice.

Regardless of whether your oral is in the form of a prepared speech followed by questions or entirely questions and answers, look frequently at your graders. If you get nervous looking directly into their faces, pick out a point somewhere in their midst and look at that. They'll think you're looking at them.

If you're expected to give a formal presentation, don't write out your speech. Work from notes. If you stand up and read a prepared speech, it will look like you don't understand your subject.

STRATEGY 5: DON'T PUT ON AIRS

Keep your language at a level at which you are comfortable. This is not the time to try to impress people with big words that you aren't sure how to pronounce or phrases that seem stiff and stilted—even to you. Instead, concentrate on sounding enthusiastic about your subject. Enthusiasm is contagious; it's a great grade-raiser.

STRATEGY 6: TREAT QUESTIONS SERIOUSLY

Whether or not the questions after a formal presentation count in your grade, many oral exam graders believe that your ability to field tricky questions shows how well you really understand the topic. Here's how to handle questions.

Tactic 1: Jot down questions

If you're permitted to take notes, jot down key words

from questions. This is particularly helpful—and impressive—if the question is long or contains several parts.

Tactic 2: Size up the questions

If you're confident that you can answer all aspects of a complicated question, show off. Rephrase the question and point out that there are several possible directions you could take in answering it. Then you might ask the questioner if he or she prefers you to take one particular point of view or another. Even if you are instructed to address just one aspect, you'll get credit for knowing a great deal about the entire topic. You'll also get credit for showing confidence.

However, if you *can't* tackle all aspects of a complex question, rephrase the question orally so that it emphasizes what you know best. Then answer the part you're best prepared to handle. At the end, cover yourself by asking, "Does that answer your question?" Chances are, the questioner won't remember exactly what he or she did ask and will nod approvingly.

Tactic 3: If you don't understand something, ask

It's better to ask a questioner to clarify a question than to give what may be the wrong answer. However, whenever possible, keep control of the question *yourself.* Don't directly ask for clarification; say that you see several possible parts to the question and suggest the one part that you're most prepared to answer. Unless the questioner interrupts with a clarification, just plunge right in with your answer.

Tactic 4: Think

Don't be afraid to take a minute to organize your answer and jot down important points you want to cover. You will get more credit for your answer than if you hem and haw and filibuster and stumble out loud while you search your memory for the facts you need.

STRATEGY 7: IF YOU DON'T KNOW AN ANSWER, DON'T PANIC

If you don't know the answer to a question, say so. Also explain *why* you don't know: "That's a good question, but it's just outside the area I think I was assigned for this exam," or, "I'd like to get into that. It seems like an important area for someone to research. But it's more detailed than we've been able to get into during this course."

Whatever you do, don't panic. It's just possible that one of the oral examiners has become so interested in you and your topic that she simply wants to learn more even though she's aware that the question may be outside the scope of your expertise. If something like this happens, take it as a compliment.

STRATEGY 8: MAKE A GOOD EXIT

Keep your cool right to the end. Once the examiners dismiss you, don't hightail it out of the room. Collect your papers neatly, stand up, smile (if you can), and leave with a gracious "Thank you."

17

Open-Book and Take-Home
Exam Strategies

In order to get the most points for an open-book or take-home exam, you must understand why they're given. They are not intended to test how much you know about the subject but how well you can find, use, organize, and interpret data.

STRATEGY 1: BECOME FAMILIAR WITH THE TEXTBOOK

If you're preparing for an open-book test, learn how to find your way around in the book. Study the table of contents. Get a feel for the index by looking up a number of topics picked at random. Read the chapter or chapters on which you will be tested so that you know what's in them and what point of view the authors take on the subject. Learn how to find and use the appendices, tables, charts, and other aids the book contains.

STRATEGY 2: DON'T COPY YOUR ESSAYS OUT OF THE BOOK

A take-home essay exam is little more than an ordinary essay assignment, except that it may be worth more points. Try to find out the maximum expected length and shoot for that. Zealous students always write long take-home exams, and you don't want to be penalized for saying the same thing in fewer words. With most instructors, a long paper picks up some extra credit just for being long.

On both open-book and take-home essay exams, never copy more than a sentence or two verbatim from the textbook or other assigned reading. And whenever you *do* copy, put it in quotes and identify the source. Remember, the point of the exam is not to test how well you copy but how well you digest, explain, analyze, integrate, or add to the assigned information—in your own words. If you can add interpretations or opinions of your own, so much the better, but label them opinions if that's what they are. Work as many different sources and references as possible into your take-home essay, and mark them clearly because they're generally worth lots of extra points.

STRATEGY 3: PREPARE FOR PROBLEM-SOLVING EXAMS

Take-home and open-book exams that involve problem solving require advance preparation if you're going to do your best. You can get information from the open book, but you can't learn puzzling concepts for the first time. Make sure, before the exam, that you understand all the important principles, formulas, definitions, and so forth. Also do some open-book pretests as you prepare for the exam.

APPENDIX A

Helpful Books, Internet Sites and Software

The exam preparation books from Learning Express (www.learnatest.com) are helpful for practicing test samples, especially *1001 Math Problems, 1001 Vocabulary and Spelling Questions, 501 Challenging Logic and Reasoning Problems,* and *501 Word Analogy Questions.*

In addition, other publishers, including Kaplan, Educational Testing Service, College Board, Cliff's Notes (a division of John Wiley & Sons), and Sparknotes, offer books to help prepare for graduate school entrance exams, civil service and career exams, and high school equivalency exams. Many have sample problems, with answers, that can be used for practice in taking standardized tests. Browse through them at your local bookstore.

For tips to help you study most productively, see *Study Smarts* by Judi Kesselman-Turkel and Franklynn Peterson (2nd edition, University of Wisconsin Press, 2004).

For a current list of SAT and ACT preparation software, select Software and Search at the SuperKids site (www.superkids.com) and search for SAT. Educational Testing Service provides free and inexpensive downloadable practice software for their GRE, GMAT, and TOEFL exams at www.gre.org/pracmats.html and other linked sites. For intensive computerized math tutorials, see MathAid at www.mathaid.com.

There are many inexpensive programs that make flash cards for studying at the computer or printing out. Here are two:

FlashCard Pro: $9.95, for Windows (MicroACE Software, Atlanta, GA). A demonstration copy can be downloaded at www.memorize.com.

Flashcard Wizard: free shareware but donations are accepted. For Macintosh and PowerPC Macintosh. Can be downloaded from the Fool's Workshop at www.foolsworkshop.com.

There are also many inexpensive good speed-reading and touch-typing programs for sale. Check the listings at the website www.simplythebest.net/shareware/educational.

To find books and software that can help you study particular subjects, use your favorite search engine (ours is Google) and search for "educational + study + test + math (or chemistry or whatever other subject you need help with) + software" (or + book) and check out the first 50 hits.

TECHNICAL PAPERS FOR PARENTS AND TEACHERS

To learn more about the theories and research studies that helped provide the background for this book, we recommend the following:

Foster, Sharon K., Allene Paulk, and Barbara Riederer Dastoor, "Can We Really Teach Test-Taking Skills?" *New Horizons in Adult Education* 13, no. 1 (fall 1999).

Krasner, Steve, "Test Anxiety and Test Taking 1990-1999" (Connecticut State Department of Education, www.ctserc. org). This excellent comprehensive bibliography can be viewed online at http://www.ctserc.org/library/actualbibs/TestAnxiety.PDF.

Plake, B. S., and S. L. Wise, "Analysis of Guessing Behavior on Multiple-Choice Examinations: Between Group vs. within Group Designs," *Bulletin of the Psychonomic Society* 24 (1986): 251-53.

Taylor, C., and K. R. White, "Effects of Reinforcement and Training on Title I Students: Group Standardized Test Performance." Paper presented at the Annual Meeting of the American Educational Research Association, Los Angeles, CA, April 1981 (ED 206 655).

Wise, S. L., L. L. Barnes, A. L. Harvey, and B. S. Plake, "Effects of Computer Anxiety and Computer Experience on the Computer-Based Achievement Test Performance of College Students," *Applied Measurement in Education* 3 (1989): 235–42.

APPENDIX B

Most-Used Exam Direction Words

The following words usually have the specific meanings listed below, though there is always an instructor who means something else by them.

Compare: Show how they are the same and how they differ.

Contrast: Show how they differ.

Criticize: Examine the pros and cons and give your judgment.

Defend: Give details that prove it or show its value.

Define: Just give the meaning.

Describe: Give the details and examples that show what it is.

Discuss and *review:* Examine from all angles. (These words are catchalls. Depending on the teacher, they might mean trace, outline, describe, compare, list, explain, evaluate, defend, criticize, enumerate, summarize, or tell all you know about it.)

Distinguish: Tell how this is different from others similar to it.

Evaluate: Give your opinion as to the advantages and disadvantages.

Explain and *show:* Show, in logical sequence, how or why something happened (or both).

Illustrate: Give examples.

Justify: Give the facts and then prove it's true.

Name, list, tell, and *enumerate:* Give just the information that is specifically asked for.

Prove: Show that it is true and that its opposite is false.

Summarize and *outline:* Give the main points.

Trace: Show how something developed step by step (usually chronologically).

Other common terms, found in instructions and questions, that should be carefully read and noted are:

synonym
antonym
similar to
the same as
the opposite of
assume that
only one correct choice
all but one
if
all of
none of

APPENDIX C

How Most Ideas Are Organized Logically*

Group 1. In time sequence:
- in the sequence in which it was seen or done
- in the sequence in which it should be seen or done
- from cause to effect

Group 2. From general to specific:
- general topic to subtopics
- theoretical to practical
- generalizations to examples

Group 3. From least to most:
- easiest to most difficult
- smallest to largest
- worst to best
- weakest to strongest

---

*Reprinted from *Good Writing* by Judi Kesselman-Turkel and Franklynn Peterson (New York: Franklin Watts, 1981).

- least important to most important
- least complicated to most complicated
- least effective to most effective
- least controversial to most controversial

Group 4. From most to least:
- most known to least known
- most factual to least factual (fact to opinion)

Group 5. Giving both sides (grouped or interspersed):
- pros and cons
- similarities and differences (compare and contrast)
- assets and liabilities
- hard and easy
- bad and good
- effective and ineffective
- weak and strong
- complicated and uncomplicated
- controversial and uncontroversial

APPENDIX D

Some Common English Prefixes, Suffixes, and Roots

LATIN-DERIVED PREFIXES

Prefix	Meaning
ab	from, away, off
ad	to, toward, for
ante	before
con, com, co	with, together, together with (also used to mean *very*)
contra, counter	against, in opposition
de	down, off, away, from
dis, di, dif	apart, not, in different directions
ex, e, ef	out, out of, from, off, forth, without (also used to mean *very*)
extra	outside, outside of
in, il, im, en, ir	in, on, upon, into, toward, against, out (also used to mean *not*)

inter	between
intra, intro	within
mis	badly, bad
ob, obs, sc, of, op	to, toward, for, against, meeting, in the way, hindering, veiling (also used to mean *very*)
per, pel, par, pil	through, by (also used to mean *very*)
post	after
prae, pre	before, previous, ahead, in advance, surpassing
pro, por, pur	in front of, forth, for, instead of
re, red	back to, backward, again (also used to mean *very*)
retro	back, backward, behind
se	apart, without, aside
sub, suc, suf, sug, sup, sus	under, below, from below, lower, in secret, in addition, instead
super, sover, sur	above, over
trans, tra, tres, tre	across, over, beyond, through, into a different state or place
ultra	beyond
un	not

GREEK-DERIVED PREFIXES

Prefix	**Meaning**
a, an	not, without

amphi, amph	both, of both sides, on both sides, around
ana, an	up, upward, backward, again, anew (also used to mean *very*)
anti, ant, anth	opposite, against, rivaling, in exchange
apo, ap, aph	from, away from, off, quite
arch	chief, leading
auto	self
di, dy	two, twice
dia, di	through, between, apart, across
dys	ill, bad, difficult
ek, ex	out, out of
el, em, en	in, into
epi, ep, eph	upon, at, for (of time), to, on the ground of, in addition to
eu, ev	well, good, advantageous
homeo	similar
homo	same
hyper	over, above, beyond, exceedingly, excessive
hypo, hyp, hyph	under, below, slightly
isos	equal
kata, kat, kath	down, away, concerning, mis- (also used to mean *very*)
meta, met, meth	with, after, beyond, over, change
ortho	straight, right, true

paleo	old
para, par	beside, beyond, contrary to, amiss, irregular
peri	around, about, near
pro	before, in front of
pros	to, toward, in addition
syn, sym, syl, sys	with, along with, together, like
tri	three times

GREEK-DERIVED SUFFIXES

Suffix	Meaning
archy	rule by
cracy	rule by
ectomy	cutting out of
eum, aeum	place for
gram	thing written or drawn
graph, graphy	writing
isk	a little, little
ism	state of, attachment to, belief in, practice of
ist	one concerned with, one who adheres to, one who believes in
ite	one having to do with, inhabitant of, descendent of (also used to form names of chemicals, minerals, etc.)

itis	inflammation of
ity	quality of, state of
ium, ion	thing connected with (also used to mean *little*)
ize	to make into or like, to subject to, to put into conformity with
logy	collection of, study of, science of
m, ma, me	act of, state of, result of
mancy	foretelling by
oid	like, resembling
oma	morbid affection for
osis	process of, disease connected with
se, sis, sy	act of, state of
t, te, tes	one who, that which
ter, tery, terion	place for, means for, instrument for
tomy	cutting, cutting of
ton	thing that is
urgy	art of working

LATIN-DERIVED ROOTS

Root	Meaning
acerb	harsh, bitter
acu	needle, sharp
adipi	fat
agri, ager	field

albu	white
alt	high
amen	pleasant, charming
angu	angle, corner
anima	air, breath, life, soul
an	old woman
ann	year
apex, apic	point, top
aqua	water
arma	arms
ars, art	skill, art
artu, art	joint
ater, atri	black
aur	gold
barba	beard
bell	war, pretty
bene	well
bon	good
capit	head
carp, carpt, cerpt	pick, pluck
car	dear
cede	go, yield
cel	sky
cept, capt	take, hold, grasp

cert	sure
circ	about, around, ring
commun	common
cor, cord	heart
corp	body
cred, credit	believe
culpa	fault, blame
cura	care, trouble, attention
curv	bent, curved
dens, dent	tooth
edi	building, house
ego	I
equ	equal
estu	heat, tide
exter	outside
facie	appearance, surface, shape, face
fact	make, do
ferru	iron
ferus	wild, untamed
fest	joyful
fide	trust, faith
fini	limit, boundary, end
firm	fixed, steadfast
flor	flower

form	shape
fort	strong
fortu	fate, fortune
fum	smoke, steam
funer	death, funeral
fusc	dark
gelid	icy cold
gens, gent, genu, gener	tribe, race, kind, sort
gradu, gress, gredi	step, degree
gratu	pleasing, grateful, agreeable
grav	heavy
homo	man
hosp	host, guest
host	enemy, sacrifice
infer	under
inter, itiner	journey
ipse	self, own
iter	again
jur, jus	law, right
juv	young man, young
labor	work
latus, lati	wide
latus, later	side

laud	praise
liber	free, unrestrained
locu	place
luci	light
magn	great
mal	bad
manu	hand
mens, ment	mind
met, metu	fear
misc	mingle
miti	mild, soft
mode	measure, method, fashion
mors, mort	death
mos, mori	habit, custom
mund	earth, the world
munu, mun	duty, gift, reward
ne	not
nef	sin, impious deed
niger, nigr	black
nihil	nothing
noct	night
norm	measure, standard, pattern
noster, nostr	our
nov	new

nox	harm
null	none
omni	all
onus, oner	burden
oper	work
ops, opis	influence, wealth
ordo, ordin	order, regular succession
par, pari	equal
pars, part	portion
pauc	few
pen	nearly, almost
pes, pedis	foot
pesti	disease, plague
plan	level, flat
pleb	common people
plus, plur	more
port, portu	harbor, port
post	coming after, following
primu	first
radi	root
re, res	thing, matter
rect	upright, straight
regn	government, rule
ruber, rubri	red

sacer, sacri	sacred
sign	mark, token
solu	alone, single
somn	sleep
son	sound
suc	juice, sap, taste
super	upper
temp	time
ultra	beyond, farther, in addition
unda	wave
vacu, vanu	empty
ver	true
vet	old
vi	force
via	way, road
vir, viri	man
vita, viv	life
voci	voice

GREEK-DERIVED ROOTS

Root	Meaning
acme	point, prime
acro	topmost, outermost
aer	air

agora	assembly
algo	pain
allo	another, different
ambli	dull
aner, andro	man
ankyl	bent
antho	flower
anthropo	man
apsi	arch
archa	old, ancient
aster, astr	star
atmos	vapor
aura	breeze, breath
auto	self
baro	weight
bary	heavy
basis	step, stand
batho	depth
biblio	book
brachy	short
brady	slow
caco	bad
ceno	empty
chari	favor, thanks

chloro	light green
chroa, chroma	color
chrono	time
chryso	gold
cosmo	order, harmony, universe
crato	power
dactyl	finger
de, des	binding
dele	hurt
demo	people
derma	skin, hide
dipl	twofold, doubled
do	giving
doxa, dog	opinion, thought
ecto	outside
endo, ento	within
eon	lifetime
eos	dawn
ergo	work
eros, erot	love
eso	within
ethno	nation
etho	custom, character, nature
eury	wide

exo	outside
ge	earth
gen, gene, gon	born, become
geno	race, kind
glossa, glotta	tongue
gramma, graph	letter, something written, small weight
gymno	naked
gyne	woman
gyro	ring, circle
haem	blood
helix	spiral
hetero	other
holo	whole, entire
homalo	even, regular
homo	same
homoi	similar
hora	time, season
horo	boundary
hydro	water
hygro	moist
hypno	sleep
ichthy	fish
idea	form, kind
idio	one's own

isos	equal
kine	movement, motion
lepto	small, weak, fine
leuko	white
macro	long
mega	great
mela	black
meso	middle
micro	small
miso	hatred
mne	memory
nema	thread
neo	new
neuro	nerve
nomo	law
oligo	few
onym, onomat	name, noun
ops, opo	eye, face
ortho	straight, right, true
ox, oxy	sharp, acid
pachy	thick
pan, pant	all, every
phobo	fear
phone	voice, sound

phos, photo	light
phren	mind
phyle	tribe, race
plat, platy	broad
pneu	breath
pol	city
poly	much, many
psych	breath, life, soul, mind
pyr	fire
schis	split
sema, semato	sign
soma, somato	body
sopho	wise
tachy	swift
tauto	the same
tele	afar, from afar
telo, teleo	end
topo	place
trachy	rugged, tough